Contents

Treat this treasure if you ever decide to visit. I have marked this book with things I believe you HAVE to see. Read well.

D1571798

Food Lovers' Guide to Montana

*Best Local Specialties,
Markets, Recipes, Restaurants,
and Events*

Seabring Davis

Guilford, Connecticut

To buy books in quantity for corporate use
or incentives, call **(800) 962-0973**
or e-mail **premiums@GlobePequot.com**.

Project editor: Jessica Haberman
Layout artist: Lisa Nanamaker
Text design: Nancy Freeborn
Maps: Daniel Lloyd © Morris Book Publishing, LLC
Illustrations © Jill Butler, with additional illustrations by Carleen Moira Powell

Library of Congress Cataloging-in-Publication Data is available on file.

ISBN 978-0-7627-5428-1

Printed in the United States of America
10 9 8 7 6 5 4 3 2 1

The prices and rates listed in this guidebook were confirmed at press time. We recommend,
however, that you call establishments to obtain current information before traveling.

Russell Country (Central)

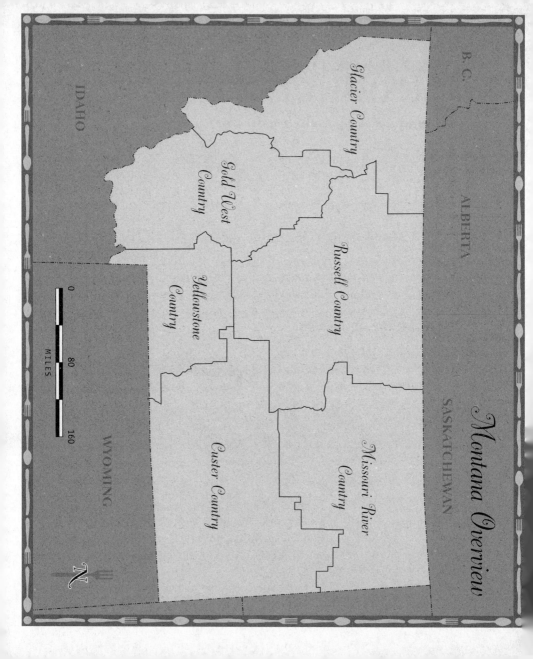

Montana Overview

B.C.

IDAHO

ALBERTA

SASKATCHEWAN

Glacier Country

Gold West Country

Russell Country

Yellowstone Country

Missouri River Country

Custer Country

WYOMING

0

80

160

MILES

N

Introduction

Let's be honest. No one has ever called Montana a gourmet food destination. It's far from the trendy world of haute cuisine, black-tie affairs, and fancy culinary techniques. Part of that is because Montana is not easy to get to: It's far north—up near Canada. And there aren't a lot of people here—less than a million. And this is a very big state for so few people—which makes it hard to keep a restaurant open.

That's not to say that the food in Montana isn't tasty, or that Montanans don't enjoy eating well. Quite the contrary. Folks around here won't hesitate to drive over 100 miles just for dinner. Some make sojourns to neighboring towns to stock up on specialty foods with a cooler and ice in tow. But what you'll find on menus in these parts is simple food, nothing gussied up, nothing too exotic. As one chef I spoke with said, "I don't use any fancy words for the stuff I make, I just use good food."

Yet, the idea of eating your way through a place is a wonderful notion. Meals are highlights of any trip, providing both sustenance and pleasure. And in many ways, eating is the best way to understand the culture of the state. How else would you learn that the rich farmland of Glacier Country has summer produce markets as abundant as any in Southern California; that the cattle ranches of the Missouri, Custer, and Yellowstone regions are peppered with German and Scandinavian heritage; that Butte, America, (as it was called in its heyday) once claimed the largest Irish-American population outside of Boston and remains the best place to celebrate St. Paddy's Day; or that the "urban" centers of Bozeman, Missoula, and Billings crave fresh, local foods, fostering a richening restaurant culture and at last some scrumptious ethnic cuisine options. You can experience all this on the menus of cafes around the state, from the vendors at festivals, at the farmers' markets, and at the specialty food shops.

You can sum up Montana's food scene, and, truthfully, the culture of the state, as well, in a couple words: simply good.

The demand for fresh, local, and organic food is growing among Montana consumers, as it is elsewhere in the nation. Yet, despite the dominance of the agricultural industry in the state, it can be challenging to find fresh foods in Montana. That's changing, however, as grassroots efforts throughout the state encourage small growers and livestock producers to market and sell their products to the public. As organizers of the Montana Farmers Union put it on their Web site (www.whoisyourfarmer.org), "It has taken more than a generation for us to distance ourselves from the source of our food. Many growers have disappeared. If you help create the demand, local farmers will eventually diversify their farms and attract the next generation of farming." Montanans spend $3 billion annually on food, but only 9 percent of that goes to food grown or processed within the state, according to the Montana Food System Council (MFSC). Fifty years ago, however, 70 percent of the food consumed in Montana was produced here; MFSC is a private, non-profit group that is working with the Departments of Agriculture, Public Health and Human Services, Commerce, Labor and Industry, and Corrections to change that fact. Thankfully, small Montana farms and ranches are on the increase in recent years. A revived interest in fresh regional food has sparked more farmers' markets, more growers, and subsequently more great eateries to respond to the demand for local food products that sustain the culture and economy of Montana. For food lovers, that translates to more fresh, healthy local cuisine that is unique to this place.

Known first as cattle country, thanks to its vast open range and grasslands, Montana produces much more than beef. Given the sheer span of miles and remoteness of the state, traditionally many of the livestock producers needed to grow their own vegetable gardens for sustenance. The emergence of modern transportation systems and a global economy after World War II have made a variety of produce more accessible in supermarkets, but thankfully some of the heirloom gardening practices of the past century are re-emerging here.

In all four directions of this vast state, it's becoming easier to skip the freezer-to-fryer road food and find something a little fresher. Regional foods emerge from a history of primarily European immigrants who settled here during the early twentieth century, thanks to American milestones that resulted from the Lewis and

Clark Discovery Expedition. Effects of he Emancipation Proclamation from the Civil War, the Homestead Act, and the push for westward expansion all created the spice of Montana, and, with a little digging, expose wonderful ethnic influences along the culinary trail.

With the area's history in mind, the chapters of this book lead you through the regions of the state, based on historical connections that have cultivated communities that yield wonderful Western flavors and open hospitality. Beginning with Yellowstone Country in the southwestern portion of the state, where Yellowstone National Park attracts the largest share of the state's visitors, we'll move up and across the state in search of gold, glaciers, big open country, cowboy artists, legendary rivers, plains, prairies, and peaks. From Yellowstone, we'll travel the trail of early miners into Gold West Country, in western Montana, and then move through the northwestern region, along the "banana belt" of Flathead Valley, and into Glacier Country, where Glacier National Park is the most prominent destination. Then we'll follow what's known as the Hi-Line into vast prairie that borders Canada, with a dip down into the central portion of the state known as Russell Country, made famous by early-twentieth-century cowboy artist C. M. Russell, who documented life on the range. From the middle of the state, we'll cover endless miles of open road into Missouri River Country, in the footsteps of Lewis and Clark's Discovery Expedition, following a trade route that has become legendary in the making of the American West. Moving southeast to the state's largest city and Custer County, where the tribes have carried on Native American traditions despite the misfortunes of history, a culture of pioneers, cowboys, and bitter battle over land stands out more starkly than anywhere else in the state. Each region bears its own culture and subtle culinary signatures that straddle the barbed wire fence that has become the West, a line that leaves one foot on the side of history and the other on the line of progress, so evident even in the food we consume, the emphasis on traditional eateries, and the emergence of trendy restaurants. Eating a trail through the state is a great way to learn about each community, and I hope you'll enjoy your tableside view of Montana.

How to Use This Book

This guide has been organized into six chapters, based on the historic geography of Montana: Yellowstone Country (Southwest), Gold West Country (West), Glacier Country (Northwest), Russell Country (Central), Missouri River Country (Northeast), and Custer Country (Southeast). Each region is vastly different, but all are steeped in an agricultural renaissance that places an important emphasis on fresh food prepared simply and deliciously. While exploring the history of this state you'll have the opportunity to sample handmade goat cheese, Welsh pasties, bison burgers, and Hutterite huckleberry wine. No doubt, traveling through these countries will be a feast. Within each chapter you'll find the following categories:

Made or Grown Here

From French chocolatiers to tamale-makers to fourth-generation cattle ranchers, this section features some of the most surprising and delectable culinary offerings you'll find anywhere. Many of these culinary artisans sell their products directly from farms or factories, by Internet and mail order, or to wholesalers or retailers in the region and around the country, whose locations are listed here.

Specialty Stores & Markets

This section offers the best sources of local and fresh ingredients for your own fabulous meals. Some may be grocery stores that feature a significant variety of regionally made foods and locally grown produce. You'll find the best sources for artisanal cheeses and sauces, coffee roasters, bakeries, and candymakers to help you seek out the best of Montana's goodies.

Farmers' Markets

Montana's farmers, ranchers, and craftspeople have done a tremendous job of organizing markets in every small town or big city from the mountains to the prairies. Most markets run from June through late September, offering seasonal produce and freshly harvested meats once or twice weekly. Some regions have embraced a homesteader's approach to growing and have organized winter markets as well, selling canned vegetables and greenhouse crops.

Farm Stands

In the most fertile sections of Montana—around Flathead Lake, for instance—cherry stands pepper every bend of the highway. In the rest of the state, however, these homespun vendors are few and far between. While not all the chapters feature this section, those that do are the jewels of the Treasure State, offering everything from delicate Flathead cherries to the sweetest corn you've tasted since crossing the hundredth meridian.

Food Happenings

There's nothing like a feast to bring food lovers together, and Montana has an abundance of celebrations, often seasonally oriented, that revolve around eating and drinking. You can follow winter microbrew fests, harvest festivals in the fall, summer food fairs on the middle of Main Street, and spring wine tastings across the state.

Landmark Eateries

Whether serving the biggest cut of premium Montana beef or the freshest crop of spring morels, the restaurants of the region cater to a wide range of tastes. Some places are worth traveling hundreds of miles to enjoy a dinner, best hamburger, or most refined pastry—and people do it! Other places are historic landmarks worth experiencing even if the food is not outstanding, while still others offer the perfect package of place and pleasure drawn from an unforgettable meal. This section will take you through the state's iconic eateries, old saloons, diners, hole-in-the-walls, and elegant dining rooms. Two special sections of the book highlight establishments that are key to Montana culture—classic steak houses and saloons.

Montana Steak Houses

Montana steak houses, also called "supper clubs" or "dinner clubs," used to be the classy restaurants for a special night on the town, where the steaks hang over the side of the plate and you can keep your cowboy hat on through dinner. Often the cuisine at these eateries isn't the fanciest or most creative, but it's simply good. It's served with old-fashioned side dishes like twice-baked potatoes, steamed broccoli, and Texas toast, or if it's a really nice restaurant, a relish tray to start you off right. Look for the icon that marks these classic cowboy restaurants.

The old saloon is where woolly Western flicks show the ultimate barroom brawl and the do-or-die gambler's bet. In some places, such as Froid or Sunburst (where the Mint Bar doubles as a church), the establishments are more community gathering places than watering holes. Some of them are legendary—near Great Falls, the Mint Saloon was where artist C.M. Russell and his friends relaxed after work. (The Paris Gibson Square Museum of Art has the original back bar on display.) The saloon provided the prolific artist the first public gallery for his works and remains one of the largest collections of his paintings today.

Usually called The Mint or The Stockman—both names are ubiquitous in Montana—the saloon is integral to the personality of each town. The former name speaks to the miners who staked claims in the early 1800s, looking for riches in the Treasure State. The latter refers to the ranching culture; the saloon was often where the stockgrowers' association members gathered. Saloons range from swanky to downright stinky, but in all, they're hard to resist once you start your mission to have a drink in every one you pass (and a designated driver to chronicle the adventure safely). Most will surprise you if you give them a chance and walk into the dimly lit room, akin to the community forum a diner might offer in any city.

Restaurant Price Key
$ = inexpensive; most entrees under $10
$$ = moderate; most entrees $10 to $20
$$$ = reasonable; most entrees $21 to $30
$$$$ = expensive; most entrees more than $30

 Learn to Cook
Some specialty stores, restaurants, and wineries offer regular cooking classes and wine courses. Some classes are offered by private chefs or professional caterers through well-established venues offered by community adult education programs.

Brewpubs & Microbreweries

With the spread of microbrews and home brewing across the country has come a new generation of brewers in Montana. Perhaps German heritage influences some of the stoutest beers made here, but more than anything, the brewmasters make what they like. From pale ale to amber, the spectrum of flavors and styles of beer is a burgeoning tradition here. Most of the bigger cities showcase an array of microbreweries and create a treasure map across the region.

Wine Trails

Surprisingly for a northern state, some regions of Montana have produced award-winning wines. Though limited by the short Zone 4 growing season, microclimates in the northwestern area see enough growing time to produce Pinot Noir, Cabernet, and Zinfandel grapes that will delight the most experienced wine lover. Yet the little-known joys of fruit wine from huckleberries and chokecherries from the eastern section of Montana will vie for your palate in a fun-loving way. This isn't a wine snob tour; it's more of a homegrown picnic basket of sweet diversion. Look to our chapters on Glacier Country and Missouri River Country for information on wineries.

Recipes

Peppering the pages of this book are delectable recipes that reflect some of the culture of Montana. It's a collection from the state's chefs, farmers, and fellow food lovers. I am grateful to the restaurants and growers who graciously provided them. The recipes are adapted for home preparation in a standard kitchen. Get cookin' and savor a taste of Montana in every bite.

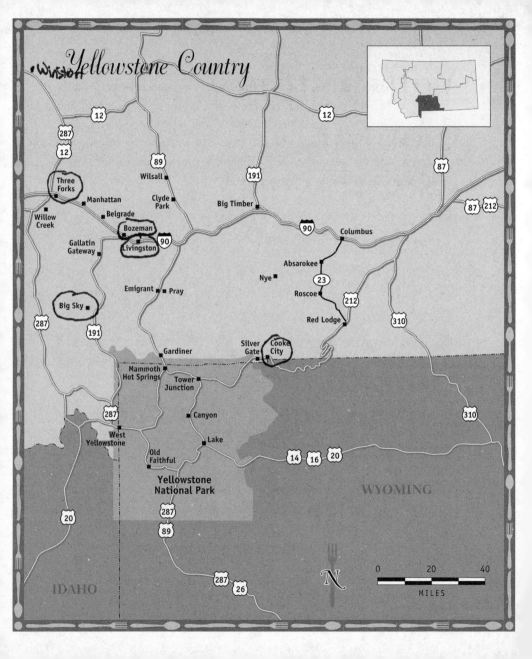

Yellowstone Country (Southwest)

The idea of having Yellowstone National Park (the world's first national park) as your backyard is appealing to many folks, and so many interesting towns center around its gateways. With the population come perks for foodies, from restaurants to farms to markets, and a fresh food renaissance in this part of the state. The communities that have taken root at the edges of Yellowstone likely experience the greatest influx of seasonal visitors, and the lively mix of events, quaint historic downtown areas, interesting eateries, and entertainment reflect this fact.

Although restaurants may be few and far between in the wilds of Yellowstone, look to the variety of farmers' markets and specialty shops to stock up for preparation of good meals while camping out during the summer. You'll also find locally made products in convenience stores, or c-stores, and regional grocery stores.

For travelers, Yellowstone Country is generally a two-season destination: summer and winter. In this region, Bozeman and the Gallatin Valley gather the largest population. The area is so fertile that it was known as the "Valley of the Flowers" by the many Northern Plains tribes who migrated through the region. It remains agriculturally productive, with large wheat and potato farms, cattle ranches, and small but versatile sustainability-centered gardens. Outlying gateways to Yellowstone Park, such as Big Sky, Gardiner, Red Lodge, West Yellowstone, and Cooke City, cater to the strong summer and winter visitor months, but increasingly more towns are active all year round. Just take any exit off Interstate 90 and you'll find some of Montana's most engaging small towns; this is where the authentic experiences begin.

Made or Grown Here

Amaltheia Organic Dairy, 3380 Penwell Bridge Rd., Belgrade; (406) 388-5950; www.amaltheiadairy.com. The name "Amaltheia" comes from Greek mythology, and it refers to the goat that nursed Zeus. Its horn gave us the cornucopia. Amaltheia is family-owned and operated, and its goat cheese dairy is certified organic and purely Montana made. The rich and creamy chèvre, ricotta, and feta are memorable and can be found at local grocers and specialty food stores.

Farmers Melvyn and Sue Brown began the Amaltheia Dairy in 2000. They started milking with ninety goats. The operation started small, as they gauged consumer interest. What they found was a niche for artisanal cheeses made locally; in 2002, the Browns decided to develop and begin operating their own cheese facility. Through trial and error, they developed exceptional products that speak for themselves through the texture and flavor of their handcrafted cheeses. Today they are milking about 280 goats, producing 150 gallons of goat milk each day, and selling product to more that 50 retailers in the state and nationwide at Trader Joe's. Amaltheia produces and stocks the finest and freshest all-natural cheeses, supplying many fine restaurants and supermarkets. Visitors are welcome to tour the facility; call to confirm tour times.

B Bar Ranch, 1273 Otter Creek Rd., Big Timber; (406) 932-4197. Wes Henthorne operates this family-owned ranch, raising Ancient White Park cattle that are certified organic, grass-fed, humanely raised, chemical-free, and hormone-free. The result is healthy, tender, good-tasting meat that is available at Good Earth Market in Billings and Bozeman Community Food Co-Op, among other locations.

Béquet Confections, 8235 Huffine Ln., Bozeman; (406) 586-2191; www.bequetconfections.com. Making caramels started as a hobby for Robin Béquet. It was the highlight of her gift-giving during the holidays, when she set up her home kitchen into what grew into a tremendous production year after year, as her list of friends and family lengthened. When her twenty-five-year career in technology sales management and business management ended with the telecom crash of 2001, she pursued her passion for fine confections with full attention. The recipes were simple at first—smooth, buttery caramel with just the right chewy texture, and people loved them. She started marketing the candy in Bozeman and quickly branched out to retailers across the country. The recipes became bolder: in 2007 Béquet Confections won an award at a national food show for the Chipotle caramel. Now, with 650 clients and a brisk mail-order business, Béquet has a splendid array of flavors, from pomegranate to Celtic sea salt to black licorice. It didn't hurt that she received great press from *Martha Stewart Living* and *Food & Wine* magazines in recent years, but the proof of success is in the confections. How sweet it is!

Since then, her creamy caramels have been showcased on the Food Network and in *Martha Stewart Living*, heralded for their soft, buttery delicacy. There are ten delectable flavors; the most unusual are black licorice, pomegranate, and chipotle. (This author's favorite is the Celtic Sea Salt.) The business is based in Bozeman, but more than 650 gourmet markets and natural food stores across the country carry Béquet Gourmet Caramel. Call (877) 423-7838 for retail locations near you, or look for the caramels locally at Bozeman Community Food Co-Op, Joe's Parkway, Oak Street Market, Chico Hot Springs Resort, and other locations.

Country Classic Dairies, 1001 North Seventh Ave., Bozeman; (406) 586-5425; www.countryclassic.com. On the shelves at any grocery store in Montana or Wyoming, the Country Classic label for milk products, butter, and yogurt sits next to the more expensive certified organic brands. Country Classic Dairies is a dairy cooperative established in 1932 that produces hormone-free milk (cream, heavy cream, and buttermilk, too), processed locally. More than one hundred family farms from western Montana and the surrounding region contribute to the product.

Henry's Sauce & Condiment Company, 405 Stillwater Ave., Bozeman; (406) 585-3376; www.henryscatsup.com. A neighbor's thoughtful gift of overripe tomatoes spurred Matt Henry and his wife, Sue, to try out Henry's Grandma Bish's homemade ketchup. After the first few batches, they simplified the process by starting with pureed tomatoes. That led to an actual business, as friends and family begged for more ketchup; today the tangy-sweet sauce is available at many specialty food stores and directly from the company on their Web site.

Indreland Ranch Angus Beef, 170 Glasston Rd., Big Timber; (866) 901-BEEF (2333) or (406) 932-4232; www.indrelandranch angusbeef.com. When it comes to beef, ranch owners Roger and Betsy Indreland ask you these questions: Are you concerned about food safety? Do you want to know where your food comes from? Do you want beef with no added growth hormones?

Simple queries in this complicated world where foodborne illnesses have become a frequent headline. The Indrelands asked themselves the same questions and modeled their traditional cattle ranch as an answer. In turn, they sell natural beef at farmers' markets in Big

FARM AND RANCH TOURS

Find out where your meat and potatoes come from on one of the state's unusual agricultural tours. It's not quite as difficult to make it on the farm as it was back in 1862, during the original homesteader days, but you can get a firsthand experience of living off the land. Many ranches offer guest quarters, dude ranching opportunities, and scheduled private fishing. Here are a couple in Yellowstone Country:

Ferry Creek Ranch, 177 Old Clyde Park Rd., Livingston; (406) 222-4835. Owned by the Forstenzer family, this 560-acre ranch is located on the Yellowstone River near Livingston. Raising certified organic, grass-finished Galloway beef, Ferry Creek Ranch supplies stores in Billings, Bozeman, Helena, Great Falls, and Missoula. One of Montana's oldest operating ranches, Ferry Creek Ranch has many of its buildings listed on the National Historic Register. The Granary, a charming two-bedroom cottage, is available for rent.

Timber, Billings, Bozeman, and Livingston, as well as to numerous restaurants in the state. Look for their meat on menus at Bridge Creek Backcountry Bar and Kitchen in Red Lodge, at Montana Aleworks in Bozeman, and at Yellowstone National Park Lodges as you travel. Alternatively, you can order your own package of beef for your freezer at home. Either way, the taste of these naturally aged cuts of meat make any effort to obtain them worthwhile.

MZBar (MZ-) Cattle Company, 5805 Dry Creek Rd., Belgrade; (406) 388-4180; www.milesnickrecreation.com. Tom and Mary Kay Milesnick's land appears more like a wildlife refuge than a ranch, as mallards, pheasants, herons, pelicans, white-tailed deer, and sandhill cranes call it home, along with the 500 head of cattle. As operators of the MZBar (MZ-) Cattle Company, the Milesnicks are the third generation of their family to ranch in Gallatin Valley and they pride themselves on managing the land with its natural resources in mind. The ranch's 1,400 acres are located on rich bottomland with access to plenty of water. In fact, the East Gallatin River, Thompson Creek, and Benhart Creek flow through the productive crop and pastureland on the MZ-, offering an unusual spring creek fishing experience for anglers. Reservations are required.

For a complete listing of agricultural tours throughout Montana, go to the state travel Web site: www.visitmt.com/experiences/food_and_beverage/farmers_markets/agtour.htm.

King's Cupboard, P.O. Box 27, Red Lodge; (800) 962-6555; www.kingscupboard.com. The manufacturing plant is located in Red Lodge, but you'll find King's Cupboard's extensive line of specialty products, chiefly Montana-made items, all over the state. What began as two people working in a small kitchen has branched out to a thriving twenty-person business. Lila Randolph-Poore and Rigger Poore started small with a test kitchen in 1990. Their company has been featured on the Food Network and in *Food & Wine, Bon Appétit,* and *Better Homes & Gardens,* among others.

The first recipes came from Lila's grandmother's kitchen, but all have been tested extensively to make a home cook's life very easy. The chocolate sauce is rich and creamy as a topping on any flavor of

Baked Brie with Caramel Sauce

1 wheel of Brie
1 11-ounce jar King's Cupboard
    Caramel Sauce
Puff pastry dough (Pepperidge
    Farm is recommended)
Toasted pecans or almonds
    (optional)

King's Cupboard
P.O. Box 27, Red Lodge
(800) 962-6555
www.kingscupboard.com

1. Preheat oven to 400°F.
2. Remove Brie from packaging.
3. Microwave caramel sauce for about 20 seconds or until spreadable.
4. Spread caramel sauce on top and sides of Brie wheel. Reserve some caramel for drizzling later.
5. Wrap Brie in puff pastry (following the manufacturer's directions) and bake for about 20 minutes, or until puff pastry has browned.
6. Drizzle remaining caramel on top of pastry.
7. Garnish with toasted pecans or almonds if desired.
8. Serve with crackers, bread, or fruit.

Serves 6 as an appetizer.

ice cream, but it's the Molten Chocolate Cake Mix that I've returned to over the last decade. (At dinner parties I try to pass off these decadent chocolate bombs as my own, though my guests are rarely fooled.) It seems I'm not the only one, as the King's Cupboard factory produces as many as 5,000 boxes of mix for these cakes with the gooey center each day.

Miller Farm Natural Pork, 1106 West Park St., Livingston; (406) 220-1939. That maxim about "the other white meat" doesn't quite apply with the deluxe cuts of pork from Miller Farm. Unlike the typical grocery store pork, this meat has *fat,* but in a good way, in a way that makes a person remember that food should be savory and succulent. Whether it is the tenderloin, steak, ribs, bratwurst, or pulled pork sandwiches, Miller Farm has become known in the area for its wonderfully tasty offerings. The products are fixtures at local farmers' markets, county fairs, natural food stores, and during the holidays at a booth in the Gallatin Valley Mall (beginning around Thanksgiving). Family-run and locally owned, the business is managed by Leah Miller, who guarantees quality and consistency and markets her family's products in a low-key manner that exudes small-town hospitality.

Montana Hunting Company, 412 Pronghorn Trail, Bozeman; (406) 585-9042; www.montanabuffalomeat.com. For a true Western experience, consider harvesting your own buffalo. Montana Hunting Company hosts bison hunts and harvests on Montana's premier bison and wildlife ranch, the historic Flying D. Fill the freezer with delicious, grass-fed, low-fat meat, and take home the robes and skulls that will provide lasting memories of the experience. Hunters have their choice of a trophy bull bison, management bull (when available), or cow bison. Hunts are for rifle and archery hunters. The average trophy bison is seven to twelve years old and will score high in the Safari Club International record book.

The 113,593-acre property is a working ranch managed for the production of bison and wildlife. It's the Old West and New West rolled into one, a working model for restoring native species to superb natural habitat in southwestern Montana.

Montana Monster Munchies, P.O. Box 10711, Bozeman; (800) 752-2158; www.mtmonstermunchies.com. Montana Monster Munchies of Bozeman touts its product as "The Last Best Cookie," and it's hard to disagree. These giant cookies are filled with all-natural goodness—oats, raisins, chocolate chips. They became the fixture for sweet tooths around here twenty years ago and are found at concessionaires in Yellowstone National Park, countless coffee shops, convenience stores, and markets, as well as by mail order in all fifty states.

Roughstock Distillery, 705 Osterman Dr., Suite C, Bozeman; (406) 579-3986; www.montanawhiskey.com. This Bozeman distillery jump-started in 2008 and bottled its first batch of Montana whiskey in fall 2009. Owned and operated by Montana natives Bryan and Kari Schultz, the distillery has produced a smooth, amber single malt using Montana barley, distilled in copper and aged in new oak barrels. At the tasting room (coming soon) you can belly up to the bar for a two-ounce sample of their barrel and buy one bottle to take with you. It is also served at Plonk in Bozeman and sold at Montana Wine and Spirits in Bozeman. Give it a shot!

Senorita's Specialty Foods, 116 East Main St., Manhattan; (406) 284-3180; www.senoritasspecialtyfoods.com. Established in 1989, this Manhattan, Montana, company produces a line of sauces and salsas that are mouthwateringly memorable. Look for these fresh products in grocery stores and locally owned markets from one end of the state to the other. The company first made a splash selling its signature salsas at farmers' markets. Habañero salsa is *hot,* but along with the heat it has a wonderful flavor. It is a light, refreshing salsa, with a hint of jalapeño. Or try the sweet and hot flavor of the Caribbean, great as a condiment on your Thanksgiving turkey or on venison roast, or a tangy hot salsa verde (made with tomatillos). Additionally, Senorita's offers two types of pesto: Classic basil pesto, made with Montana-grown organic basil, roasted pumpkin seeds, and pine nuts, has a wonderful mild flavor. The sun-dried tomato pesto has roasted almonds.

Sterling's Lamb, 170 Old Clyde Park Rd., Livingston; (406) 222-7219. Colette Stewart's family ranch near Livingston raises natural lamb to supply restaurants and markets in the region. Frozen chops, racks, boneless legs, and other cuts are sold. Custom orders and delivery are available, but the ranch also sells at the Livingston farmers' market from June through September.

Wheat Montana's Whole Wheat Banana Bread

½ cup (1 stick) butter or margarine

1 cup sugar

2 eggs, lightly beaten

1 cup mashed banana

1 cup Wheat Montana Natural White flour, unsifted

½ teaspoon salt

1 teaspoon baking soda

1 cup Wheat Montana Prairie Gold whole wheat flour, unsifted

⅓ cup hot water

½ cup chopped nuts

1. Preheat oven to 325°F.
2. Melt butter and blend in sugar.
3. Mix in beaten eggs and mashed banana and blend until smooth.
4. Stir together white flour, salt, baking soda, and whole wheat flour, then add dry ingredients alternately with hot water to banana mixture.
5. Stir in chopped nuts.
6. Spoon batter into greased 9 x 5-inch loaf pan.
7. Bake for 70 minutes until golden brown or insert a toothpick in the center; if it comes out clean the bread is done.
8. Cool in pan for 10 minutes, then turn on rack to finish cooling.

Makes 1 loaf.

Wheat Montana Bakeries and Delis

10778 Highway 287, Three Forks
(406) 285-3614
www.wheatmontana.com

Wheat Montana Bakeries and Delis, 10778 Highway 287, Three Forks; (406) 285-3614; www.wheatmontana. com. Makers of wholesome all-natural breads baked with grains harvested from the family farm, Wheat Montana is a staple of any grocery store within the Rocky Mountains. Family-owned by the Folkvords—they have been involved in agriculture for three genera- tions—Wheat Montana has operations that encompass 12,000 acres of the most productive soil in Montana. Located near the headwaters of the Missouri River, near the town of Three Forks and 5,000 feet above sea level, it is also the highest elevation at which grain is grown in North America. The Gallatin Valley facility includes grain cleaning and processing, flour milling, and a full- scale bakery that services a five-state area. The grains, cereal, and flour are sold nationwide. Wheat Montana Farms has also made its way into *Guinness Book of World Records* for cutting, milling, mixing, and baking a loaf of bread in 8 minutes and 13 seconds! In 1999 *Food & Wine* named the Wheat Montana hot dog bun the best for making the perfect hot dog. They make a great sticky-bun cinnamon roll, too! Wheat Montana has eight locally owned bakery and deli outlets in the state, so you should be able to find some of the freshest bread around.

Wilcoxson's Ice Cream, 314 South Main St., Livingston; (406) 222-2370. Made in Montana since 1912, Wilcoxson's ice cream comes from manufacturing facilities in Livingston and Billings, Montana. The company has grown greatly since its humble beginnings in the

Wheat Montana's Old-Fashioned Seven-Grain Cookies

3 eggs, well beaten
1 cup raisins
1 teaspoon vanilla extract
1 cup (2 sticks) butter
1 cup brown sugar
1 cup white sugar

2½ cups Wheat Montana Natural White Flour
1 teaspoon salt
1 teaspoon ground cinnamon
2 teaspoons baking soda
2 cups Wheat Montana 7-Grain Cereal

1. Preheat oven to 350°F.
2. Combine eggs, raisins, and vanilla, and let stand approximately 1 hour covered.
3. Cream together butter and sugars.
4. Add flour, salt, cinnamon, and baking soda to sugar mixture. Mix well.
5. Blend in egg-raisin mixture and 7-Grain Cereal. Dough should be stiff.
6. Drop by heaping teaspoons onto ungreased cookie sheets. Bake for 10 minutes or until lightly brown.

Makes 6 dozen cookies.

Wheat Montana Bakeries and Delis
10778 Highway 287, Three Forks
(406) 285-3614
www.wheatmontana.com

back of the Wilcoxson's Candy Store in Livingston. Today Wilcoxson's services most of the towns and large cities in Montana, northern Wyoming, and Yellowstone National Park. Look for Montana Moose Moss (mint chocolate chip) or the best-selling Moosetracks (vanilla ice cream with peanut butter cups and chocolate chips) and a variety of ice cream bars, sold everywhere from convenience stores to the finest local restaurants.

Specialty Stores & Markets

All Things Italian, 2251 West Kagy Suite 1, Bozeman; (406) 586-0444; www.all-things-italian.com. This specialty food shop for the Italianophile is a small market-style store that focuses on authentic Italian products—wine, beer, cured meats, imported cheese, olive oil, vinegar, pasta, sauces, condiments, confections, coffee, linens, pottery—and occasional cooking classes. The store is the culmination of a dream that mother-daughter team Connie Anderson and Nichole Joyce decided to pursue together. Putting their love of Italian food and cooking together, each day they offer prepared lunches that range from Italian-style hearty soups to panini to pasta in limited quantities or made-to-order (twenty-four hours ahead) for larger groups. The shop also offers premade dinners for those of us who are too busy to cook. The menu varies daily.

All Things Italian Spinach and Ricotta—Stuffed Cannelloni

1 24-ounce jar tomato and basil pasta sauce

2 cups whole milk ricotta

1 egg

1⅔ cups grated Parmigiano-Reggiano

20 ounces fresh spinach, cooked, drained well, and chopped

2 tablespoons butter, melted

Sea salt and freshly ground pepper

1 box De Cecco no-boil cannelloni*

1 cup shredded Asiago cheese

*Available at All Things Italian

1. Preheat the oven to 375°F.
2. Butter or spray the bottom of a 9 x 13-inch baking pan. Spread a thin layer of tomato sauce in the bottom of the baking dish.
3. Stir together the ricotta, egg, and 1 cup of Parmigiano until smooth.
4. Fold in the spinach and melted butter.
5. Season with sea salt and pepper and mix until blended. Transfer filling to a pastry bag or a zippered bag.
6. Pipe filling into the cannelloni shells and layer in the bottom of the pan. Spoon the rest of the tomato sauce over the shells and sprinkle on the shredded Asiago cheese and the rest of the Parmigiano.
7. Cover with foil and bake for 30 minutes, then remove foil and cook another 5–10 minutes, or until cheese is golden brown.

Serves 6–8.

All Things Italian
2251 West Kagy Suite 1, Bozeman
(406) 586-0444
www.all-things-italian.com

Babcock & Miles, Ltd, 105 West 12th St., Red Lodge; (406) 446-1796; www.babcockandmiles.com. "Merchants of the delectable" is their slogan, and it's enough to tempt any foodie through the door. Karen and Andrew Porth, a physician and her architect husband, transplanted their lives to Montana... and also their taste. This tiny mountain town is lucky to have a gourmet food shop that offers a wide assortment of cheeses, crackers, charcuterie, antipasti, oils, vinegars, coffees and teas, specialty sauces, and beautiful cuts of frozen duck breast, rabbit, and veal chops. A diverse selection of wines—from sake to Sangiovese—is also available. The shop is just a jog off Broadway, the town's main drag, and it's the perfect place to assemble a gourmet picnic basket du jour to take on a scenic drive up the Beartooth Highway or into Yellowstone Park.

Bagelworks, 708 West Main St., Bozeman; (406) 585-1727; www.bozemanbagelworks.com. For bagels, this is the only show in town. Since 1991, the staff has been boiling and baking New York–style bagels. Though this is far from a New York City deli, the texture and taste of a Bagelworks specialty is a wonderful substitute. In addition to bagels that are crisp on the outside and doughy inside, Bagelworks offers blends of specialty cream cheeses to order or in ten-ounce containers to go. The best seller is Bagelworks' blend of lox cream cheese, but this foodie's favorite combination is the honey walnut cream cheese on a cinnamon raisin bagel or, when I'm eating alone, the chive cream cheese on a garlicky "Works" bagel.

Bagelworks products are also sold at the Bozeman Community Food Co-Op, but they are best straight from the shop—grab a baker's dozen and you're good to go for the day.

Chalet Market, 6410 Jackrabbit Ln., Belgrade; (406) 388-4687; www.chaletmarket.com. Chalet Market is best known for its gourmet jerky and sausage (try the Buffalo Salami), available in specialty food stores from California to Oklahoma. In Belgrade, Chalet sells its own products in a retail gift shop and deli. In the shop you can find a great sandwich, homemade soups and salads, buffalo and elk jerky, summer sausages, and snack stix, all made on the premises. In the gift shop are many Made in Montana products, along with a wide selection of microbrews from Montana and all over the world.

Opened in 1976, Chalet Market is an innovative effort by ranchers who saw the need for an outlet to sell their meat locally. Only the savviest locals know the word on this Swiss-inspired building outside of Belgrade on the way to Big Sky; look for the buffalo sign and then turn in for some savory treats.

Chocolate Moose Candy Store and Soda Fountain, 140 East Main St., Bozeman; (406) 551-2148. This old-fashioned candy store and soda fountain in downtown Bozeman opened its doors in a newly renovated historic building in 2009. Owner Tammy Hauer was inspired by the nostalgia of 1950s-style malt shops. The store is a whimsical bit of all things sweet: barrels of bulk candy, freshly pulled taffy, cotton candy, and an old-fashioned soda fountain at the counter. The soda fountain's sodas, milkshakes, and malts are all made by hand with locally made chocolate selections on a specially built soda fountain machine shipped from Chicago.

Coffee Factory Roasters, 6½ South Broadway, Red Lodge; (406) 446-3200. There's nothing like the aroma of roasting coffee beans, and this neighborhood shop has all the right olfactory triggers. The Beartooth Blend, roasted here weekly, is a robust, mellow coffee that is a favorite around the state. The atmosphere here is light and airy, with a big window looking onto the town's main street. There's Wi-Fi and good coffeehouse chatter.

Community Food Co-Op, 908 West Main St., Bozeman; (406) 587-4039; www.bozo.coop. This natural food market and cafe is jokingly referred to as "the food museum" because everything in the place is just so beautiful. But seriously, folks, the Co-Op has been a resource for food lovers in the area since 1979. With the slogan, "Be a yokel, buy local," it is the place to find the widest selection of produce, meats, dairy products, and condiments made or grown in Montana (and within 300 miles of the state borders), as well as organic products, bulk goods, and vitamin supplements. The take-out lunch counter, fish market, and salad bar are stocked with delicious and abundant dishes for lunch or dinner. Upstairs at the Flying C Café, outstanding housemade muffins, scones, desserts, cookies, smoothies, coffee, and tea drinks are served in a casual atmosphere that looks out over the bustle of Main Street, to the Bridger Mountain Range.

Eagle's Store, 3 Canyon Street, West Yellowstone; (406) 646-9300; www.eagles-store.com. Walking into the old soda fountain at Eagle's Store is a nostalgic excursion. A West Yellowstone landmark, Eagle's has been family-run since 1908, offering a complete line of fishing tackle, backpacking equipment, and hiking boots, and an outstanding line of Western wear. It is one of the original businesses in iconic West Yellowstone, sharing a border with the famous national park.

General manager Karen Eagle can tell stories of working as a fountain girl in the shop when she and her cousin Kendra were kids in the 1970s and of her family's recollections of their years here. "It's the kind of place people return to," says Karen, the granddaughter of founders Sam and Ida Eagle. "I hear people sit at the soda fountain telling their kids about their own memories of grandfathers bringing them here."

Aside from its history, one of Eagle's signature attractions remains the old-fashioned soda fountain. Its back bar was acquired in 1910—its exact age is unknown. The front tiled counter was added early in 1930; the original leather is on all of the stools save five. Sundaes and malts are made with real ice cream and homemade chocolate sauce. While you are there, take home a jar of Mom Eagle's Homemade Chocolate Sauce, a recipe that has been passed down from Ida Eagle to her daughters and granddaughters.

Elle's Belles Bakery and Café, 7 Tai Ln., Bozeman; (406) 587-5683; www.ellesbellescookies.com. First known for her voice on the local radio station KMMS 95.1 as a DJ and diva, then for her cottage cookie industry, proprietor Elle Fine mixed all of her talents together into one great recipe. Her brownies and cookies made with love are sold throughout Bozeman at these businesses: MacKenzie River's Bozeman stores, La Parilla, the Naked Noodle, Joe's Parkway Market, Dave's Sushi, Rockford Coffee, the Bean Machine, and at Elle's Belles Café, of course. Throughout the year, the cafe hosts music and events for the public. On Wednesday, Thursday, and Friday nights from May through September, you can call for cookie delivery on what Elle calls "crazy good ooey-gooey Chocolate Chip Hot Cookie Nights." Hard to beat fresh cookies at the doorstep!

Fishtail General Store, 35 Main St., Fishtail; (406) 328-4260; www.fishtailgeneralstore.com. It's a funny thing to list a "general" store in a "specialty" section, but the truth is that this is one of the few remaining on what was once the open frontier. Like a pioneer mercantile, Fishtail General Store has a little bit of everything—and that makes it unique. On the way to Red Lodge and eventually, the Beartooth Pass, off Highway 90 at the Columbus exit and then south on Highway 419 about 21 miles, it's worth a stop for lunch. A century ago Fishtail General Store was a gathering place for a scattered rural community, and it remains the same today. The store gives a nod to nostalgia, with an authentic decor that includes hardwood floors, shelves of dry goods, and the original building that housed the store back in 1900, as well as serving 10-cent ice cream cones to kids nine and under. The local mercantile store was where folks went for almost everything they needed—food staples like flour and sugar; meat (which was butchered right there in the store); clothing, shoes, hardware, and housewares; animal feed; and so on. Just as in days gone by, when there was a butcher, a baker, and a candlestick maker all under one roof, Fishtail continues the tradition. This is the kind of place where you can order your steaks cut to your desired thickness and find the "Fishtail General Store Special Sausage," a delicacy treasured by regular customers. You can also order lunch at the deli, stock up on other groceries, and buy hardware for your DIY home projects, as well as get the last odds and ends of camping, hunting, and fishing supplies, including hunting and fishing licenses.

Foodworks, 421 East Park St., Livingston; (406) 222-8223. Tucked into an innocuous strip mall between the community thrift store and a popular casino, this gem of a natural food store has a strong local clientele. In addition to offering peanut and almond butter grinders in the bulk food department, this is the place to find fresh locally grown produce all year round. Vitamin supplements, baked goods from local bakeries, or chocolates from the sweetest confectioners in the region, Foodworks hails to the healthy side of all of us.

The Gourmet Cellar, 212 West Park St., Livingston; (406) 222-5418; www.thegourmetcellar.com. The Gourmet Cellar is a jewel in the historic crown of Livingston—the classic Burlington Northern Depot that anchors the town. From her idyllic shop, Debbie Endres has cultivated a loyal clientele for her wine and cheese club and specialty store. In a town where every restaurant lists some cut of beef on its menu, Debbie carries over 400 wines, in all price ranges, from Spain, France, and Italy, along with many South American, South African, and Australian selections, and, of course, a wide variety of wines from California and the Pacific Northwest. She hand sells nearly every bottle and offers educated advice on the wines she represents. That's all good, but what is even better about the Gourmet Cellar is the selection of artisanal cheeses, both domestic (some local) and imported, all delectable. My mouth waters even as I write the names of her selections: Perlagrigia, Manchego, Humboldt Fog, Bleu d'Auvergne, Pondhopper. A fresh rotation of cheeses arrives weekly and it's worth visiting regularly to discover something new. Debbie also carries a splendid array of specialty foods, pastas, sauces, condiments, and chocolates from around the globe, along with a distinct lineup of microbrews and select imported beers.

Heeb's East Main Grocery, 544 East Main St., Bozeman; (406) 586-5464. Locally owned by Mitch Bradley, Heeb's has been a downtown Bozeman institution for close to fifty years. Some swear it has the best meat department in town. Run like an old-time butcher shop, Heeb's offers meats of premium quality. Many products are Montana-raised and the service is excellent. Heeb's other attribute, according to locals, is that its location encourages folks to shop at their neighborhood store, just like in the good old days.

Hungry Moose Market and Deli, 11 Skywood Rd., Big Sky; (406) 995-3045; www.hungrymoose.com. Nothing beats a Breakfast

Biscuit sandwich grabbed from the Hungry Moose and eaten while making the drive up the mountain to Big Sky Resort's leg-burner ski runs (kids: don't try this at home). Fresh baked biscuits and a concoction of eggs, green onions, and sausage are great fuel for a day on the slopes. Owners Jackie and Mark Robin opened this mountain market in 1994 when the only other place to buy groceries in Big Sky was the Conoco station off Highway 191. Not only is this the place to shop for groceries, but it's a local hangout for espressos and deli sandwiches. From wine to wild huckleberry brownie mix, Hungry Moose stocks it. They even offer a grocery delivery service for a small fee and online shopping if you are just getting off the hill at Big Sky and don't have time to shop.

Joe's Parkway Market, 903 West College, Bozeman; (406) 586-2005; www.joesparkway.com. Although it's located across from Montana State University freshman dorm buildings, this is more than a college students' convenience store. Joe's does tout the fact that they have "Beer, beer and more beer!" for the university chugging set, but the selection of microbrews, imported wine, and hand-cut artisanal cheese is world-class here. In addition to specialty foods, there is also a deli and select meat department, as well as an ample fresh produce department. They do still sell Ramen noodles, however, so the college kids aren't forced into gourmet life.

La Chatelaine Chocolate Co., 1516 West Main St., Bozeman; (406) 522-5440; www.chatelainechocolate.com. Owners Shannon and Wlady Grochowski refer to their chocolaterie as a "Frenchy little chocolate shop." She grew up in Mississippi and he was raised in Paris (yes, France), but they share a love for cooking and together bring French sophistication to sweet treats. Combining flavors such as jasmine, lavender, and green tea into handmade truffles and ganache, each luxurious bite is a morsel to be savored. The little shop where the chocolates are made is tucked off the beaten path on East Olive and is easily missed, but the aromas of exotic chocolates that permeate the store make it worth seeking out. The more visible satellite location is downtown in the Baxter Hotel building lobby, outside Ted's Montana Grill, on the corner of South Willson Ave., and West Main St.

Leaf and Bean, 35 West Main St., Bozeman; (406) 587-1580; and Bridger Peaks Town Center, 1500 North 19th St., Bozeman; (406) 587-2132; www.leaf-bean.com. The Bean's claim to fame is the fact that it is Bozeman's oldest coffeehouse. More than twenty-five years ago (before the double skinny, half-caf, vanilla-flavored latte craze and well before the Chai cravings began), this espresso joint and gourmet tea shop was the hip place to hang. Kate Wiggins has cultivated a strong following first with the original downtown location in the historic Hawthorne building and then at a more contemporary location in a shopping center off the North 19th commercial corridor. Both locations have walls hung with a rotation of works from local artists and host a slew of events each month, from folk music to poetry readings and writer's gatherings. The baked goods are phenomenal (don't pass on the lemon bars) and the selection of hearty cold sandwiches will instill a regular hankering for the roast turkey with apricot mayo on ciabatta bread. Mmmm!

Montana Candy Emporium, 7 South Broadway, Red Lodge; (406) 446-1119. Bins and barrels full of candy are tagged with handwritten signs showing old-fashioned names: Walnettos, B.B. Bats, Kits, Snaps, Ice Cubes, Squirrel Nut Zippers, Black Jacks, Fizzies. Open since 1991 and offering more than 800 different candies, Montana Candy Emporium may be the state's largest candy store. The owners have done everything possible to make a stop at their store feel like a step back in time to an early 1900s mercantile. The shop is filled to the gills with collectible and nostalgic gewgaws, from antique bicycles to a working nickelodeon. It's sensory overload at its sweetest. The emporium is located in the historic Park Theater building; it's impossible to miss the classic marquee sign advertising Squirrel Zippers.

Montana Fish Company, 119 East Main St., Bozeman; (406) 556-0200. The old adage "never eat seafood if you are more than one hundred miles from the ocean" was clearly composed before the advent of overnight shipping. Montana Fish Company flies fresh fish in daily; both the quality and the absence of a fishy stench are proof of this fact. Located in historic downtown Bozeman, this little shop supplies many local restaurants with seafood and also does a clipping retail business, offering seasonally fresh oysters; clams;

ahi tuna; mahi, king, and coho salmon; halibut; and so much more. Montana Fish prepares sushi to go for the downtown business lunch set and also features a good selection of small-vintage wines. Home cooks, buy the "secret sauce" as an accompaniment to your catch of the day; it's mixed in small batches here and will make your fish ultra delish.

Oak Street Natural Market, 1735 West Oak St., Bozeman; (406) 582-5400; www.oakstreetnaturalmarket.com. This is a natural food store where you can buy organic, local produce along with a variety of vitamin supplements and eco-beauty products. But the best thing about Oak Street Natural Market is the deli. Vegetarians flock here (along with meat lovers) for creative concoctions such as the BCT Melt with brie, chutney (mango–passionfruit), and honey-roasted turkey on a circle croissant. There's a selection of hot panini (my favorite is the Portobella, a great mix of marinated portobello mushrooms and grilled sweet red and yellow peppers, grilled organic red onions, sautéed organic spinach, and garlic Gorgonzola cheese on La Brea focaccia). Robert Worobec and his wife, Linda Terry (who also owns Livingston's Foodworks), pride themselves on offering healthy foods that are delicious, but the real star here is Bettie Shomper, who dishes out some of the savoriest health food in the state.

On the Rise, 1001 West Main St., Bozeman; (406) 582-0272; www.wordofmouthconcepts.com. This little bakery is built around a 24-ton, brick wood-fired oven that masterfully cranks out artisan breads that are perfectly crusty on the outside and ideally doughy on the inside. The place to go when a friend asks you to bring some bread for dinner, as well as the choice of many local restaurants and groceries, On the Rise serves naturally leavened organic European-style breads that range from basic farmer's loaves of France to the ciabatta of Italy, a Flemish version of sourdough, as well as breakfast sweets, herbed breads, pizzas, and too much more to list. Head baker Sheryl Dahl loves to talk about the zen of baking and surely coined the shop's motto: Bake bread, not war.

Plonk, 29 East Main St., Bozeman; (406) 587-2170; www.plonk wine.com. Urban hip meets Bozeman's cowtown Main Street at last—at least in this swanky wine bar. Inarguably *cool,* both for its well-designed interior and for its diverse wine list, this is the place to be for wine lovers in Bozeman. Serving an array of imported vintages—Spain and Argentina seem to be on the tip of partner Bret Evje's tongue—along with classics from France and Italy, Plonk offers an impressive wine list (also available for retail sale at a 20 percent discount from the menu). My suggestion would be to belly up to the tall skinny tables across from the bar, sample some of the wines by the glass, and then purchase a bottle of your favorite to go. And if *terroir* is not your thing, this is the place for some of the finest handcrafted cocktails this side of New York City.

Rocky Mountain Roasting Company, 777 East Main St., Bozeman; (800) 428-5282; www.rockymountainroasting.com. With three locations in Bozeman and one in Belgrade (as well as one in Helena, in Gold West Country), the RMR Company coffee shops have become a mainstay for java lovers in Montana. What started in 1992 with one shop that attracted loafing college students soon grew into a stronger retail and wholesale business. Owners Hal and Cristina Berg began with a simple goal: to serve good coffee. Going strong in their second decade of the business, they now sell an array of custom-roasted coffees, among other products. At the RMR shops (and in all major stores in Montana) look for their brand of whole-bean coffees with labels that represent this state well: Old Faithful Blend, Grizzly, Jim Bridger, Yellowstone, Big Sky, and Dry Fly. Each has a unique taste, from spicy sweet to dark and smoky; you'll have to decide which is your favorite.

Rustic Candy Shop, 29 Canyon St., West Yellowstone; (406) 646-7538. Walking down the boardwalk of West Yellowstone's characteristic street, how could you resist the sweet, syrupy scent of homemade saltwater taffy? At the Rustic Candy Shop, you'll be drawn in for a treat and find fudge, caramel corn, brittles, caramels, specialty chocolates, and an assortment of fine candies that will make you feel like a giddy kid.

The Wine Gallery, 2320 West Main St., Bozeman; (406) 586-8828. The owner of the Wine Gallery, Doug Badenoch, is very passionate and wine-savvy. He's taken the Bozeman retail wine scene to a new level by offering great service and being approachable to all levels of wine enthusiasts. His column in the *Bozeman Daily*

BUTCHER SHOPS

Big Sky Premium Meats, 67 Cherry Avenue at Four Corners, Bozeman; (406) 582-9191. Touting a selection of local beef, pork, lamb, bison, and wild game, plus an impressive section of specialty foods and artisanal cheeses, this is a gourmet butcher shop that has risen to the sophisticated palates of the day. Also offering turkey, duck, and goose purchased from two local Hutterite colonies, this shop is a must for special occasions and every-night feasts for the home cook. There is also a well-curated section for beer and wine to peruse for the perfect pairing.

Matt's Old Fashioned Butcher Shop & Deli, 405 North 8th St., Livingston; (406) 222-5160. On an out-of-the-way street sits one of the finest butchers in the state, a Livingston institution at that location since 1996. The shop has won countless awards for charcuterie—sausage, jerky, smoked meats—and is a locals' pride and joy. Whether it's the custom smoked turkey sandwich you take for a fly-fishing picnic (Matt packs tomatoes on the side so they won't make the bread soggy

Chronicle often expresses just who he is: a guy who loves wine. His monthly wine club is a perfect way to introduce neophytes to wine, and for the true wine snobs, it's a fun avenue for restocking the cellar with good pours. In the store, Doug offers a limited selection of specialty foods, featuring sausage and cheddar cheese from Belgrade's Chalet Market and pâté, among a few other choices that may pair well with your wine of the day.

and won't forget a real kosher pickle), the whole smoked chicken (also great for picnics!), the robust flavor of his curry lamb sausages, or the assurance that you are buying a prime cut of beef, Matt's is truly about quality. Matt trained for three years under the guidance of a German butcher and is simply passionate about food.

Some folks ask Matt why he doesn't move the shop to a more visible location, but North 8th St., works just fine, especially when hunting season arrives and the animal carcasses that need to be processed in fall and winter start rolling in. Matt's is the first choice for most area hunters and guides; he processes game meat with visions of delicious meals in each package.

The Meat Shoppe, 722 North Rouse Ave., Bozeman; (406) 586-6328. Whether it's for an everyday meal or a holiday dinner, the Meat Shoppe offers a wonderful selection of kosher meats. Tucked out of the way in an old Bozeman neighborhood, away from the hubbub of downtown, this is where a local group special-orders 200 pounds of corned beef for the annual St. Patrick's Day celebration and where you could simply get a special cut of Montana-raised beef for dinner.

Vino per Tutti, 315 East Main St., Bozeman; (406) 586-8138; www.vinopertutti.com. Forget the tarot cards; the organization system based on "personality" here just may reveal more about you than any fortune teller. Uniquely categorized according to definitions devised by owners Tim and Beverly Christiansen (no doubt under the influence of many glasses of wine), the wines at this store are of eight types: vivacious, innocent, charming, opulent,

Hunting and Gathering

This state is a paradise for people who love the outdoors, and if there is one way that the foodie and the recreationist can combine their two passions, it is in the hunt and harvesting of wild game. Known for supreme elk hunting habitat in the mountains, trophy-sized antelope and mule deer in the eastern ranchlands, and abundant whitetail deer in the pastures of the western portion of the state, Montana makes hunting an annual ritual for many families and visitors. It is big business and an important part of the cultural fabric of the state.

As a result, meat-processing plants in Montana range from specialty butcher shops to bare-bones (pardon the pun) facilities experienced with basic, clean meatpacking. Those butchers who have taken their skills to an artisanal level, offering their own charcuterie, are in high demand both with savvy hunters and home cooks. Here is a resource list for meat processors throughout the state:

Northwest Montana

Alta Vista Meat Company
4422 Highway 2 North, Troy
(406) 295-2510

Frey's Meat & Custom Cutting
2925 Highway 206, Columbia
Falls
(406) 892-2226

Lower Valley Processing Co.
2115 Lower Valley Rd., Kalispell
(406) 752-2846

Tobacco Valley Meats
582 Osloski Rd., Eureka
(406) 297-2611

Vandevanter Meats, Inc.
180 Trap Rd., Columbia Falls
(406) 892-5643

Western Montana

H&H Meats
1801 South Ave., W, Missoula
(406) 549-1483

Hamilton Packing Inc
692 Highway 93 North, Hamilton
(406) 961-3861

Hi Country Beef Jerky
1 Lincoln Gulch Rd., Lincoln
(406) 362-4203

Lolo Locker
6220 Caras Ln., Lolo
(406) 273-3876

North American Foods of Montana
333 Marcus St., Hamilton
(406) 363-1505

Valley Processing
3609 Eastside Highway, Stevensville
(406) 777-5684

Western Meats Wild Game Processing
820 Dewey Blvd., Butte
(406) 494-7514
www.stocktonoutfitters.com

Southwest Montana

Budget Game Processing
4110 Thorpe Rd., Belgrade
(406) 388-4691

Forcella Meats
33 Forcella Rd., Whitehall
(406) 287-3756

Gallatin Meat Processing
120 Pine Butte Rd., Bozeman
(406) 587-5335

Happel's Clean Cut Meat Service
4700 Gooch Hill Rd., Bozeman
(406) 587-8972

Roberts Packing Company
1086 Highway 91 South, Dillon
(406) 683-5542

Sheep Mountain Meat Processing
37 Convict Grade Rd.,
Livingston
(406) 222-4929

Tizer Meats
3558 Tizer Rd., Helena
(406) 442-3096

Top of the Hill Wild Game Processing
2900 Pioneer Mountain Scenic Byway, Polaris
(406) 834-3533

Yellowstone Processing
74 Chestnut Rd., Bozeman
(406) 587-9385

North Central Montana

5-D Processing
302 7th Ave. Southwest, Choteau
(406) 466-5835

Cascade Meat Processors
1 1st St. North, Cascade
(406) 468-9290

Chaon's Game Processing
400 4th Ave. South, Great Falls
(406) 761-2855

House of Meats Game Processing
1201 10th Ave. North, Great Falls
(406) 727-7849

Pierce Meat Cutting
415 East Main St., White Sulphur Springs
(406) 547-3467

Sportsman's Wild Game Processing
3501 Bootlegger Trail, Great Falls
(406) 452-1222

Tri-City Taxidermy & Wild Game
4125 2nd Ave. North, Great Falls
(406) 453-5575

South Central Montana

Big Timber Meats
209 East 1st Ave., Big Timber
(406) 932-5324

Sage Brush Meats
302 South 27th St., Billings
(406) 245-4161
www.sagebrushmeats.com

Skip's Critter Cutting
7119 Yellowstone Trail, Huntley
(406) 348-2309

Trails End Meat Processing
1419 Old Hardin Rd., Billings
(406) 252-5599

Northeast Montana

Big Flat Meat Co.
9710 West Endloop, Hogeland
(406) 379-2623

Hi Line Meats
behind Grain Growers Exxon on
Highway 2, Glasgow
(406) 263-2879

Hoch Meat Processing
Highway 250, Wolf Point
(406) 392-5533

North Country Meats
6195 Bullhook Rd., Havre
(406) 395-4036

Rocky Mountain Packing
500 1st St., Havre
(406) 265-3401

Treasure Trail Processing
1064 Highway 2 West, Glasgow
(406) 228-9011

Southeast Montana

Broadus Meats
Highway 212 West, Broadus
(406) 436-2204

Craig's Meat Processing Plant
Highway 16, Savage
(406) 776-2447

This list was compiled from the Montana Outdoors Directory Web site, a publication issued by the Montana Fish Wildlife and Parks Department for recreationists: www.montanaoutdoorsdirectory.com/directory/meat_processing.htm.

candid, elegant, intense, and indulgent. If you considered wine subjective before, just wait until you experience Vino per Tutti.

At the same time, this is a wonderful way to disarm the intimidation factor often associated with choosing a fine wine. At Vino per Tutti you'll find wines from all over the world, but if you're looking for standard scores assigned by magazine wine gurus, you're in for a surprise. For instance, Orin Swift Winery's 2005 "The Prisoner" Zinfandel was ranked 93 in the venerable *Wine Spectator* magazine, and at Vino per Tutti it falls into the "indulgent" category, where the biggest, boldest wines are grouped by a sense of passion for big flavorful wines rather than by a numerical score.

"Neither of us are what might be considered 'wine geeks,'" confesses Tim. "We both enjoy wine and learning about wine, and most importantly, we love helping our customers find a product that they enjoy. Drinking wine is easy; finding great wine values can be hard work. We are more than happy to do all the hard work so our customers can have a wonderful glass of wine."

Farmers' Markets

Belgrade Farmers' Market, 10 East Main St., Belgrade. Saturday 9 a.m. to 12 noon, May through September.

 Big Sky Farmers' Market, Fire Pit Park at Town Center, Big Sky. Every other Thursday from 5 to 7 p.m., July through September.

Big Timber Farmers' Market, in the parking lot of the Grand Hotel, McLeod and 2nd St., Big Timber. Saturday 9 a.m. to noon, July through September.

Bogert Farmers' Market, Bogert Park, Bozeman. Tuesday 5 to 8 p.m., June through September.

Bozeman Winter Farmer's Market, Emerson Center for Arts and Culture Ballroom, Bozeman. Every other Saturday 10 a.m. to 1 p.m., February through May.

Gallatin Gateway Farmer's Market, Gallatin Gateway Inn, Highway 191, Bozeman. Tuesday 3 to 7 p.m., July through September.

Gallatin Valley Farmer's Market, Fairgrounds Pavilion, Bozeman. Saturday 9 a.m. to noon, July through September.

Livingston Farmer's Market, Sacajawea Park at Miles Park Bandshell, Yellowstone St. and River Dr., Livingston. Wednesday 4:30 to 7:30 p.m., June through September.

Manhattan Farmer's Market, in the center of town by Railroad Park on West Main St., Manhattan. Wednesday 4:30 to 7:30 p.m., June through September.

Shields Valley Farmer's Market, City Park, Clyde Park. Saturday 9 a.m. to noon, July through August.

Livingston Roadside Fruit Sellers, West Park St. and North Ave., Livingston. Growers from Washington set up a truck to sell peaches, raspberries, blueberries, and sometimes Flathead cherries in August.

Rocky Creek Farm, 34297 Frontage Rd., Bozeman; (406) 585-0225. Located 4 miles east of Bozeman on the frontage road, Rocky Creek Farm is best known for its fall pumpkin patch (September through October). Groups of kids descend upon the cornfields to find the perfect pumpkin for a jack-o'-lantern. Visitors enjoy scenic rides on tractor-pulled trailers to the pumpkin patch, where they can choose from gourds ranging from basic orange to white and green varieties and varying from golf ball to boulder size. Inside the barn, fall gourds, squash, and homemade apple cider are on offer. The pumpkin patch is open from 9 a.m. to 6 p.m. on weekends, and from 2 p.m. to 6 p.m. (or by appointment) on weekdays.

From July through August, Rocky Creek offers fresh corn, green beans, assorted veggies, and vibrant sunflower bouquets at the farm and also at a stand along the road in Livingston (on West Park Street, in front of the Pamida store).

Food Happenings

JANUARY

Wine and Powder, Big Sky. Best Western Buck's T-4 Lodge; (406) 995-4111; www.buckst4.com. California's well-known winemaker Jed Steele has a love for Montana and returns each year to Big Sky to host a dinner and wine pairing at Buck's T-4. This award-winning restaurant matches a gourmet five-course dinner with wines from Steele Winery.

FEBRUARY

Sweet Tooth Ball, Bozeman. Emerson Center, 111 South Grand Ave.; (406) 587-0681. A benefit for women's health at Bridger Clinic, the Sweet Tooth Ball is all about chocolate and dancing. Desserts and dance lessons (ballroom) are included in the ticket price.

International Street Food Bazaar, Bozeman; (406) 994-4031. Take a gourmet trip around the world in a day at the annual International Street, Food Bazaar. This exciting intercultural gathering brings together the sights, sounds, scents, and flavors of homemade cuisine from more than twenty-five different countries. Montana State University students prepare traditional dishes from their home countries for several thousand people who come to savor the makeshift street market atmosphere on the MSU campus. Music and a variety of entertainment complete the springtime festivities that have been bringing cultures together for nearly thirty years. Small entry fee ($1–3), plus individual booth prices ($0.50–2 per portion).

MAY

Annual Farm Fair at Brainard Ranch, Manhattan; (406) 388-1616; www.belgradechamber.org. Held each May at the Brainard Ranch, Farm Fair is an opportunity to understand the origins of our foods and how they end up at the dinner table. Farm Fair is a continuing-education program of the Gallatin Valley Agriculture Committee of the Belgrade and Bozeman Chambers of Commerce. It is conducted over two days, offering students, teachers, and school administrators lessons about agricultural production, economics, soil science, animal science, and environment management, and exposing them to careers in ag-related fields. The curriculum includes water cycles, soils, weed identification, irrigation and soil conservation, forestry, beef cattle, dairy and milking cows, dairy goats and cheese, sheep, Gallatin Valley crops, farm safety, "tin can" ice cream, pleasure horses, hogs, potatoes, poultry, and the story of wheat and draft horses.

JUNE

Chili Cook-off, Big Sky. Meadow Village Pavilion, Meadow Village; (406) 995-2742. You be the judge as thirty contestants compete to make the best chili in Big Sky. Don't be surprised if the winning entry includes elk or venison. Put on your Western duds and enjoy an evening of good food, music, a raffle, and an auction of art items to benefit the Big Sky Community Foundation.

JULY

Big Sky Food Festival, Big Sky; (406) 995-4111. Local restaurants collaborate at Big Sky's Buck's T-4 Lodge for an evening of great food in celebration of summer. Each restaurant provides tasting portions that showcase the best its menu has to offer. The festival is a great opportunity to experience a cross section of the local restaurants and decide which will be your favorite. The event is held outside at Buck's T-4 Lodge. Admission is $5 per person; hours are 5 to 9 p.m.

Lunch on the Lawn, Bozeman. Emerson Center for the Arts & Culture, 111 South Grand Ave.; (406) 587-9797. The Emerson Center's Lunch on the Lawn is a Bozeman summertime tradition, Wednesdays in July and August, from 11:30 a.m. to 1:30 p.m. Bring your own lunch or splurge on hot lunch—an array of cuisines including barbecue, sweet treats, and fresh-squeezed lemonade— and enjoy this community concert series that attracts an audience of 100 to 200 people every week. The music is free.

AUGUST

Gardiner's Annual Brewfest, Gardiner; (406) 848-7971; www .gardinerchamber.com. Around Yellowstone's famous Roosevelt Arch, master brewers offer their best tastes from local microbreweries, along with burgers and brats to go with an evening of music. Festivities begin around 3 p.m. and go until dusk settles on the remarkable mountain setting.

Sweet Pea Festival, Bozeman. Sweet Pea Festival is more of a music and arts festival than a food-centered one, but it's home of the Tater Pig and so much more...

Each year, during the first weekend in August, Bozeman's summer crescendo is Sweet Pea Festival, a three-day music and arts celebration that also dishes up foods that have become part of local tradition. The festival is held in Lindley Park on East Main Street, and offers multiple stages, which may simultaneously be hosting live music (jazz, blues, rock, country, swing), a Shakespearean play, ballet, belly dancing, and live storytelling. And amidst the artful mayhem, the 10,000 or so revelers need to eat. A row of food stands (all operated by volunteers to raise money for local nonprofit groups) offer everything from smoothies, burritos, and pizza to the Tater Pig—that's a baked potato filled with a specially made pork sausage and topped with butter, sour cream, bacon bits, and chives. Mmm! What's not to love? (If you're a vegetarian, ask for a Tater Pig with no squeal: potato with everything but the sausage and the bacon bits.) The Chord Rustler's Barbershop Chorus mans the booth that sells 7,200 each year at the festival and has been doing it for the last thirty years. It's for a good cause. Most of the money raised ($6,000) will be used to send seventy-five children to the Big Sky

Youth Harmony Rendezvous, an a cappella singing camp held each year in Livingston.

Bite of Bozeman, Bozeman. As part of the Sweet Pea Festival celebration, downtown Bozeman shuts down the historic section of Main Street, from Rouse to Willson Avenues, to serve up the town's best dishes. Lining the sidewalks, food vendors from local restaurants, catering companies, and private chefs grill, fry, and freeze some of the tastiest samplings of food this side of the Continental Divide. Main Street becomes a walking food fest, much like a street bazaar.

Festival of Nations, Red Lodge; (888) 281-0625; www.festival ofnations.us. During the frontier era, Red Lodge and its mines attracted people from all over the world who came to improve their living conditions and chances for a future. From Finland came mine workers and construction workers. "Finn Town" on the east side of Red Lodge still has many traces of their unique architecture and the indispensable saunas. From the Balkans came strong laborers who did much of the heavy work and tended many of the town's shops. Immigrants from England, Ireland, and Scotland spread over all the mining districts of Montana. Italians and Germans came west, too. The last major immigrant group was the Norwegians. Their carpentry handiwork can be seen everywhere in Red Lodge's splendid architectural detail. The town's multicultural heritage is celebrated today in the Festival of Nations, held in the early part of August every year. The festivities start with an All-Nations Gala at the civic center, followed by a food-tasting event at the Wells Fargo Bank Patio in historic downtown. The celebration continues into the evening with folk music, dance, and plenty of culture.

✡**Manhattan Potato Festival,** Manhattan. Railroad Park; (406) 284-4162; www.manhattanmontana.com. It doesn't say it on the Montana license plate, but just so you know, Gallatin Valley is spud country. About 20 miles outside of Bozeman, the loop through Amsterdam, Churchill, Manhattan, and Belgrade is home to a tradition of Dutch, German, and Norwegian farmers who have kept the region anchored in seed potato production.

Imagine the Potato Festival possibilities: French fries, curly fries, buffalo fries, mashed, whipped, baked, boiled, broiled, roasted, twice-baked, stuffed, creamed, tater tots, pancakes, hash, hash browns, shoestring, latkes, salt potatoes, smashed potatoes, au gratin, scalloped, dilled, croquettes, frittata, kugel, pockets, soufflé, salad, doughnuts. Look for all these and more at this event.

SEPTEMBER

Belgrade Fall Festival, Belgrade; (406) 388-1616; www.bel gradechamber.org. The Fall Festival parade begins on Saturday morning, moving down Main Street, while the scent of grilling meat wafts through town. The meat for Saturday's mouthwatering barbecue (beginning at noon) starts cooking at the Fire Hall the day before and is the signal that the festival is about to begin. The Saturday barbecue includes a baron of beef roasted over a spit to the tune of 1,200 pounds of meat and many side dishes prepared and served by community volunteers for the town's biggest event of the year. The arts and crafts show opens in Lewis and Clark Park at 11 a.m. The homespun atmosphere and authentic small town vibe make a visit well worth it.

OCTOBER

Harvest Celebration Dinner, Livingston; (406) 222-0730; www.westernsustainabilityexchange.org. This Western Sustainability Exchange fund-raiser brings together chefs, culinary professionals, and food lovers from across the region. It's an affair for foodies designed to showcase and celebrate the region's abundance of fresh, sustainable, local foods and the families that produce them. The premier dinner and auction offers menu items from twenty or more chefs and growers. The food is phenomenal and plentiful. The Harvest Dinner has been held at Chico Hot Springs Resort in the past, but it may move to a different venue. Late September or early October.

DECEMBER

Wines of the Year Dinner, Bridge Creek Backcountry Kitchen and Wine Bar, Red Lodge; (406) 446-9900; www.eatfooddrinkwine .com. New Year's Eve at this snowy little hamlet at the end of the road sounds idyllic. Make reservations for the December 31 private party where Peter Christe and chef Eric Traeger pair their favorite wines of the year with a six-course feast.

Landmark Eateries

Beartooth Café, 14 Main St., Cooke City; (406) 838-2475; www .beartoothcafe.com; $$. The collage of candid photos plastered to one wall near the kitchen at the Beartooth Cafe captures the spirit of this eatery—it's all about fun. Order a Montana microbrew (from a hundred different choices) and the smoked trout salad (they also have great steaks) and lounge on the deck out front (in summer). Take in one of the best mountain views in Montana—the cafe looks out onto Pilot, Index, and Republic Peaks, which tower above town at an elevation around 10,000 feet.

Bridge Creek Backcountry Kitchen and Wine Bar, 116 South Broadway, Red Lodge; (406) 446-9900; www.eatfooddrinkwine.com; $$$. Putting a casual spin on upscale gourmet without sacrificing the good things, owner Peter Christe's restaurant is decorated

Dining Out . . . Literally

During the winter months, Big Sky is a wonderland worth braving for some of the most memorable picnics you'll ever experience.

Lone Mountain Ranch Sleigh Ride Dinners, 750 Lone Mountain Ranch Rd., Big Sky; (406) 995-2783; www .lonemountainranch.com; $$$$. Horse-drawn sleighs take diners to the ranch's remote North Fork cabin, where a prime rib dinner is cooked on an old-fashioned woodstove. The meal is served by lantern light and accompanied by a live guitar or mandolin player picking through a mellow litany of tunes. By reservation only.

Montana Backcountry Adventures, 2900 Juniper Dr., Big Sky; (406) 995-3880; www.skimba.com; $$$$. This ski and snowboard guide service also offers private dinners in its backcountry lodge: The Montana Dinner Yurt. Guests are transported up the slopes via snowcat to a hearty feast and music continuing into the late evening, until the moonlit ride back down the north side of Lone Mountain.

320 Guest Ranch, 205 Buffalo Horn Creek, Big Sky; (800) 243-0320 or (406) 995-4283; www.320ranch.com; $$$$. One of the area's classic dude ranches, the 320 offers sleigh rides (and wagon rides in during summer and fall) pulled by their team of beautiful Percheron horses. Set along the Gallatin River, the evening ride meanders to a campsite with a crackling fire, cowboy chili, hot toddies, and stories of life on the ranch.

with regional topographical maps—in accord with the backcountry culture of hikers and skiers that seek out Bridge Creek. Yet this is no backwoods joint: This is fine dining and it's exquisitely done with fresh, local ingredients, from beef to lamb to salad greens. Everything on the menu is commendable, but this food lover has a weakness for the crème brûlée of the day—don't pass up the lavender if it's offered.

Bugaboo Café, 47995 Gallatin Rd., Highway 191, Big Sky; (406) 995-3350; $$. "A subtle combination of rustic and contemporary" describes the style of food here as much as it does the restaurant's decor. Avid skiers, chefs, and owners Paul and Kim Cameron named their place after the mountain range in British Columbia (also known as heliskier heaven) to reflect their true love of adventure. The classic American cuisine they serve is a little less adventurous but always hardy and straightforward. Try the Bacon-Wrapped Pork Tenderloin or the comfort food-y Chicken Pot Pie for something memorably savory.

Café Regis, 206 West 16th St., Red Lodge; (406) 446-1941; www .caferegis.com; $. Friends Martha and Nancy reclaimed the classic 50s-style Regis Grocery building and created an eatery that is *the* breakfast spot in Red Lodge. Serving straight from the garden next door during the temperate months and the greenhouse in the winter, this is no greasy spoon. If your luck is on, strawberry rhubarb French toast might be the special du jour. Vegetarians will appreciate offerings such as Curried Tofu Scramble, Tofu Burrito,

Heaping Bowl (of fried potatoes), and the Number 1, an omelet that is offered veggie, with Canadian bacon, or "The Works."

Campfire Lodge Resort Café, 155 Campfire Ln., off Highway 287, en route to Hebgen Lake; (406) 646-7258; www.campfirelodge westyellowstone.com; $. This charming little red log cabin sits on the Madison River and serves the best (and biggest) pancakes within a hundred miles. It's the perfect spot to grab a hearty dinner before heading out for adventures on the water. Enough said.

Chico Hot Springs, 1 Old Chico Rd., Pray; (800) HOT-WADA (468-9232) or (406) 333-4933; www.chicohotsprings.com; $$$. South of Livingston and sort of on the way to Yellowstone National Park—if you are the type who doesn't mind a little diversion on the way to your ultimate destination—Chico has been attracting visitors for its hot springs and hospitality for over a century.

In more recent history, however, Mike and Eve Art purchased the resort in 1973. What began as a family project for the Arts years ago has become a favorite retreat for thousands of people who visit each year. And the success started in the dining room: They began by flying in fresh seafood, serving sophisticated continental cuisine, and spreading the word that Chico Hot Springs was unlike any other place in the area. Gradually they fixed up the property and grew the business. Now, on any given night, the restaurant is full. In the dead of winter. In the bloom of spring. On the hottest summer night or the shortest autumn evening. It doesn't matter that the place is a little out of the way—people find it and then

Chico's Pine Nut—Crusted Halibut

Pine Nut Crust
2 cups pine nuts
¾ cup bread crumbs
1 teaspoon salt
⅓ cup parsley

Mango Salsa
1 mango, peeled, seeded, and diced
½ small red onion, diced
½ red bell pepper, diced
½ cup chopped chives
3 tablespoons raspberry vinegar

2 tablespoons honey
2 tablespoons chopped cilantro

Port Wine Butter Sauce
2 cups port wine
½ cup heavy whipping cream
½ cup (1 stick) butter

Halibut
1 cup buttermilk
½ cup flour
4 6-ounce halibut fillets
1 teaspoon olive oil

1. **Pine Nut Crust:** In a food processor, combine all ingredients. Pulse until nuts are chopped, but not too finely; remove nut mixture and set aside. You can also prepare the crust by hand; be sure to chop the nuts before combining them with the other ingredients.
2. **Mango Salsa:** Mix all ingredients together in a bowl and refrigerate until needed.
3. **Port Wine Butter Sauce:** The butter sauce cannot be reheated or chilled, so prepare it while the main course is in the oven or just before. Reduce port over medium heat until it forms a syrup

(about 20 minutes). When it coats a metal spoon, it is ready. Add cream and reduce until thick. Remove from heat and add butter, stirring constantly until melted and smooth. Hold sauce over low heat and use promptly.

4. **Halibut:** Preheat the oven to 400°F. Place buttermilk, flour, and pine nut crust in separate bowls and arrange in a line on the counter. Take fillets and dip one side only in flour, then buttermilk, then pine nuts. On the stove heat a pan with a touch of olive oil and, crust-side down, sauté the fish until nuts are golden brown. Place the sautéed fish in a greased baking dish, bare-side down, and bake in the oven for 8 to 10 minutes. The underside of the fish will be flaky and the fillet will be firm to the touch.

5. Present the halibut in a pool of Port Wine Butter Sauce, topped with fresh Mango Salsa.

Serves 4.

Chico Hot Springs
1 Old Chico Rd., Pray
(800) HOT-WADA (468-9232) or
(406) 333-4933
www.chicohotsprings.com

they keep coming back. *Forbes Traveler* magazine recently ranked Chico's wine list one of the top ten in the country. People drive hundreds of miles to enjoy a meal and a soak at this iconic Montana getaway spot.

Chico's offers up Western hospitality with an elegant flair. It begins with a classic menu of hearty entrees: filet mignon, prime rib, beef Wellington, and seasonally fresh fish. But it doesn't end there. The spirit of the place is in the details: the dining room clad in barnwood reclaimed from buildings in the valley, a year-round geothermal greenhouse fed by hot spring runoff, and a vegetable garden to supply fresh greens for the main dining room. The long-time staff is loyal and friendly and the place has modernized seamlessly, adding amenities like Wi-Fi, a spa, and upscale hotel rooms without losing its quirky character.

Damascos Pizzeria and Spaghetteria, 90 West Madison Ave., Suite C, Belgrade; (406) 388-2724; $$. Verifiably the only oven-fired pizzas à la Roma within 300 miles. These thin-crust pizzas are meant as a first course Italian-style, but you'll find them generous enough to be a complete meal. The "Bianca," or white pizza, section offers light alternatives to our American heavily tomato-sauced pies. The nearly all-Italian wine list makes it easy to daydream an escape to Italy over the course of the meal, especially if owner Tomasso pops out from behind the kitchen counter to talk of his home in Italy and journey to Montana. The housemade pasta (an added option with every menu item) has excellent al dente texture. You'll crave the lamb meatballs in white wine sauce for months after leaving this little ristorante tucked off the main drag to anywhere. The place is easy to miss, but it's hard to forget once you've tried the food here.

Emerson Grill, 207 West Olive St., Bozeman; (406) 586-5247; $$$. Just off Bozeman's quaint downtown center, this restaurant is located in the Emerson Center, an historic school building that houses myriad small art galleries, artist studios, theater and dance companies, boutiques, and this fantastic restaurant. Serving northern Italian–inspired cuisine (that means heavy on roasted veggies, different types of risotto, and robust meats), Emerson Grill offers a dynamic menu of fresh, organic, and creative comfort food. Owner Robin Chopus has compiled a wine list that is interesting without being intimidating, and the waitstaff is well-schooled on the largely Italian selection. But the best part about the restaurant is the vibe exuded by this artistic ambience—try the private dining room, called the Ecce Gallery, for a group of ten to twenty guests—it doubles as an art exhibit space when the table isn't set for dinner. Oft missed because it isn't downtown, the restaurant is a local favorite. It's tough to get a table for dinner without reservations, particularly for the charming summer dining under the big pine tree.

The Grand Hotel, 139 Mccleod St., Big Timber; (406) 932-4459; www.thegrand-hotel.com; $$$. Owner Larry Edwards returned this 1890 landmark to its rightful glory, and now it anchors this breezy cow town. Offering sophisticated dishes with a Montana flair—

bacon-wrapped scallops with mango sauce and Montana buffalo tenderloin with caramelized onions and a fig-port reduction sauce are a couple classic menu items. High ceilings, Victorian style, and true Western flair combine to make this one of the region's favorite spots. For a less staid meal, belly up to the bar and try the saloon menu, where the "Western cut" prime rib is sixteen ounces!

John Bozeman's Bistro, 125 West Main St., Bozeman; (406) 587-4100; www.johnbozemansbistro.com; $$$. Bozeman's oldest continually running fine dining restaurant, the Bistro serves up a creative cuisine that is refreshing, savory, and memorable. Tyler and Carla Hill, along with partner Perry Wenzel, have crafted their own blend of gourmet cuisine that's held the hearts of Bozeman locals for over two decades. The daily "Superfood" options for vegetarians are addictive and the rest of the menu is filled with wonderfully fresh fish items (flown in regularly from both coasts) and flavor-bursting sauces, salsas, sambals—culinary creativity at its height is what this place offers, but with a casual atmosphere.

Land of Magic Dinner Club, 11060 Front St., Manhattan; (406) 284-3794; $$$. Land of Magic is set among the ramshackle houses of tiny Logan, just off I-90, and not far from the slightly bigger, but still tiny, Manhattan. Montana, that is. And everything in this cowboy-style supper club is very Montana: the steaks are bigger than dinner plates and the quality is outstanding. In the midst of trendy food places, this kind of old-timer's steak house has nearly been forgotten, but Land of Magic continues to operate with solid country panache—picture red-checked tablecloths and barnwood walls; relish trays that feature ranch dressing, radishes, raw broccoli, green onions, and pepperon-cini; a choice of potatoes (baked or fried); and steaks so tender they melt in your mouth. *Cowboys & Indians* magazine rated it one of the top twenty steak houses in the West. The clientele is a mix-ture of local ranchers (hat racks are by the front door, cowboys) and tourists who ogle the gigantic slabs of perfectly cooked meat set before them. The dining area rocks Western, replete with hundreds of brands from regional ranches that have been seared into the grain of the wooden walls. Land of Magic holds an annual branding party and steak barbecue the first Sunday in May.

Livingston Bar & Grille, 130 North Main St., Livingston; (406) 222-1866; www.livingstonbarandgrille.net; $$$. Chef and general manager Chris Armagost brings sophistication to classic American comfort food. His breezy style is reflected in the lighthearted atti-tude of the staff here, but as throughout the restaurant, there's refinement behind the casual. A big believer in using local ingredients, Armagost creates menu items layered in fla-vorful homemade sauces (demi-glace, anyone?) and designed around prod-ucts grown in the region. Besides the baseball-cut steak, I'd rec-ommend any of the house-made pasta.

Mark's In and Out Drive-in, 8th and Park Streets, Livingston; (406) 222-7744; $. Since 1954, Livingston's Mark's In and Out has served up tasty little burgers, shakes, and fries to hoards of hungry townsfolk and lucky tourists driving through on U.S. Highway 89. They park their cars and walk up to order from the menu that features the truest of American cuisine: burgers and fries. The hot dogs are foot-longs and the milkshakes are made with Wilcoxson's ice cream (made just down the street). Regular customers order a double burger (with everything, thanks), since the single patties are a bit thin. But a true regular orders a pizza burger (heavy on the cheese, please).

Current owner Scott Black has cultivated such a following with his upkeep of Mark's that each year, come April, the reopening of the restaurant is as telling as the vernal equinox: It's spring. People drive up, roll down the windows, and get ready for the season. On Friday and Saturday nights, you'll get a free side of nostalgia with your burger as the servers don roller skates and play carhop just like the good ol' days.

The Mint Bar and Café, 27 East Main St., Belgrade; (406) 388-1100; www.themintmt.com; $$$. Proprietors Jay (a chef) and Mary (an interior designer) Bentley keep the personality present in this Main Street hangout, continuously operated since 1904. An extensive remodel in 1995 turned it into an icon for little Belgrade. Paying tribute to beef, ranches, and the cowboy way, the atmosphere is comfortably Western and the food quality is rock solid.

Steers mounted on the walls here offer a tip of the hat to the grandfather of Montana cattle: the Longhorn. First driven north from Texas in the 1870s by Nelson Story (an incredible feat roughly chronicled by the TV series *Lonesome Dove*), the forebears of this hearty breed made the thousand-mile drive that began Montana's famous legacy of cattle country.

Jay tosses a Cajun influence into his menu because of his love affair with New Orleans. The surprising flavors set the Mint apart from other steak places and especially emerges in dishes like the shrimp Creole and the Cajun dressing and in the offer to blacken or pepper your steak for no extra charge.

Pine Creek Café, 2496 East River Rd., Livingston; (406) 222-3628; $$. This funky little place outside of Livingston is worth the detour on Highway 89 south, both for the scenic drive of East River Road, and for the memorable rainbow trout tacos on the menu. Chef Dan Shapiro has crafted an eclectic menu with all the housemade goodness that comes from using fresh and local ingredients. Other highlights on the dinner menu are worth a taste test: the Buffalo Sloppy Joe, Elk Pasta, and Montana Whitefish.

The 1940s log cabin situated along a gentle bend of the road in Paradise Valley houses a quaint, casual restaurant and bar. In summer, the shady, screened outdoor porch is the place to be to enjoy the pleasure of a well-cooked meal. From June to early October, outdoor barbecue and live music is offered every Saturday. Just look for the retro-cool neon sign with the arrow that points to Pine Creek Lodge and Café.

The Mint Bar and Café
Shrimp Creole

Remember: SPE. Suck, peel, and eat, says proprietor and founding chef Jay Bentley of his Mint-style barbecue shrimp.

1 pound (4 sticks) butter
½ cup olive oil
2 tablespoons chopped fresh garlic
2 bay leaves
2 tablespoons fresh rosemary, crumbled
1 tablespoon dried basil
1 teaspoon dried oregano
2 tablespoons Worcestershire sauce
2 tablespoons lemon juice
2 tablespoons paprika
1 tablespoon coarsely ground black pepper
Salt to taste
2 pounds (20–25 count) shrimp, shells on

The Pollard, 2 North Broadway, Red Lodge; (406) 446-0001; www .thepollard.com; $$$. Local history looks to the Pollard Hotel as a bastion of elegance and hospitality. Barbara Pollard Sanford writes in a letter about the hotel that was run by her family from 1902 to 1946: "The dining room was a lovely room in the early days with

1. Preheat oven to 400°F.
2. Melt the butter in a large saucepan and add all of the other ingredients except the shrimp. Bring to a boil, then turn off the heat and allow the sauce mixture to cool until just warm.
3. Add the shrimp to the warm (but not hot) sauce and pour into a large baking dish. Allow the shrimp to steep in the sauce for 20–30 minutes.
4. Bake the shrimp in the oven for approximately 20 minutes, stirring occasionally to cook all of the shrimp evenly. The dish is ready when all of the shrimp have turned pink.

The shrimp should arrive at the table bubbling hot. Do not try to eat them until they have cooled. When you feel that you can eat them without burning your lips, take one by the tail, dredge it through the sauce, and suck the sauce that clings to the shell. Then peel the shrimp and repeat the same process, dredging the peeled shrimp through the herbs and spices collected on the bottom of the dish. Then eat the shrimp, and savor the wonderful essence of the flavor.

Serve with lots of bread and plenty of paper towels. Accompany the shrimp with a dry Pinot Gris or Riesling or even very cold beer.

The Mint Bar and Café
27 East Main St., Belgrade
(406) 388-1100
www.themintmt.com

Serves 4 generously.

fine furnishings, high quality hotel linens, dishes, silverware and glassware. In the early days the hotel was noted for its excellent cuisine and specialized in broiled lobsters and other dishes suitable even to the most particular gourmets."

This famous hotel and restaurant was also frequented by some notorious guests, such as William Jennings Bryan, the famed silver-tongued orator; General Miles, "the Indian Fighter"; William and Marcus Daly, the copper kings; Buffalo Bill Cody and Calamity Jane; and the noted mountain man Liver Eatin' Johnston.

Today, after a lovely restoration, the hotel and its dining room retain the historic elegance of the West at its most legendary. The Victorian-style dining room with coffered ceilings and crisp white linens is a popular dinner spot for locals and tourists. But if I could have just one meal here, I wouldn't miss the fabulous Sunday brunch (especially before a day of skiing at Red Lodge Mountain). The eggs Benedict is decadent with the house-cured Canadian bacon.

The Red Box Car, 1300 South Broadway, Red Lodge; (406) 446-2152; $. Fast food doesn't have to be homogenous to be good. This is Red Lodge's oldest restaurant, where burgers, fries, and killer milkshakes are served from a hundred-year-old train car. Operated only in the summer, the Red Box Car offers a scatter of outdoor tables set up along Rock Creek.

Second Street Bistro, 123 North 2nd St., Livingston; (406) 222-9463; www.secondstreetbistro.com; $$. It's a beautiful thing to have a neighborhood bistro; the hallmark of this one is consistency. The menu hasn't changed in five years, and that's a good thing. Locals develop a love for all the favorites: Moroccan Lamb Pillows, Scampi à la Grecque, Mediterranean Fish Stew, and Homemade Meatloaf (made of pork, beef, and veal and wrapped in apple-smoked bacon).

But I'm getting ahead of myself. Any visit to Second Street requires a cocktail hour: The list is long and original, but I love the mojitos with the Bistro's own mint-infused rum. The Bistro's claim to fame was a showcase moment on an episode of chef Anthony Bourdain's TV program *No Reservations,* which featured Livingston and local foodies.

The Stockman, 118 North Main St., Livingston; (406) 222-8455; $$. Hands down, this is the place with the best cheeseburger in town. It's thick, juicy, and cooked to temperature. The fries are hand cut in Whitehall, Montana (an hour's drive from here), and are always perfectly crispy on the outside, never greasy. On a recent visit, where all eight of us ordered some version of the quarter-pound cheeseburger and raved, the waitress told us with awe that the burgers had been featured in "that fancy food magazine with the French name." I'm not sure whether *Bon Appétit* broke the news on this good old steak house, but I'll vouch that the burgers are the best. Be forewarned, you'll have to walk through the smoky bar to get to the restaurant, but it's worth it.

Ted's Montana Grill, 105 West Main St., Bozeman; (406) 582-8600; www.teds montanagrill.com; $$$. Truth be told, the food at Ted's is a bit pedestrian, but the place deserves a mention for several reasons.

First, for the buffalo steaks, the largest variety offered in the state. Second, for the celebrity of its founder, media mogul Ted Turner, who is also the largest buffalo rancher in the country. Finally, for its location in a significant building on the corner of Bozeman's historic downtown.

Ted's is known for generous portions, hand-cut steaks, and a variety of seafood and comfort food side dishes, such as squash casserole. My recommendation is to request a seat at the bar for you and a friend (for a view of little Bozeman's big-city bustle). Then order the Caesar salad, split the bison sliders (mini burgers) and a side of fries, wash it down with an excellent vodka martini (dirty), and enjoy!

The Western Café, 443 East Main St., Bozeman; (406) 587-0436; $. This is a landmark not because it is impressive for its culinary attributes but for its authentic Western character. The Formica counter is scraped from decades of coffee mugs with bottomless refills, the breakfast is basic, the waitress calls you "honey," and pie is a staple any time of day. Plus, the cafe has the biggest, gooiest, best cinnamon rolls in town.

Willow Creek Café and Saloon, 21 North Main St., Willow Creek; (406) 285-3698; $$. "You won't find many bars in Montana that serve oysters on the half shell or chicken saltimbocca," says one faithful patron about the surprising menu at the Willow Creek Café and Saloon. Surprising, because one would assume this tiny town could scarcely attract enough customers with discerning palates.

Yet the clientele drives from Bozeman, Butte, and Big Sky to nosh on the spicy, tender barbecue ribs and (if you're like me) the heart-stoppingly good chicken-fried steak. This out-of-the-way spot is one that shouldn't be missed, particularly if you can time it on a night when local country band Montana Rose plays at the saloon. It's not the state's oldest saloon, but Willow Creek is in a 1910 building that started off as the Corner Saloon during the early days when home-steaders settled the Gallatin Valley.

Learn to Cook

Adagio: Italian Wine Dinners, 101 North Main St., Livingston; (406) 222-7400. Proprietors Jim and Gerry Liska visit Italy for a month every year, and upon their return to Montana they host a five-course dinner along with some of the unique wines they've discovered during their travels. Not so much hands-on cooking experiences as much as lessons in pairing food and wine (through experience, of course), the events at chef Jim Liska's corner trat-toria take place two or three times during the winter months.

Bridger Kitchens, 1 East Main St., Bozeman; (406) 582-5411; www.bridgerkitchens.com. This high-end cook's store doubles as a classroom for monthly cooking classes and wine tastings. Hand-rolled sushi and zingy white wines that can stand up to ginger and wasabi are the main theme for these hands-on classes for novice chefs and any kind of sushi lover. And the best part is that you get to eat everything you make. The classes are held monthly and begin at 6:30 p.m. and cost $25 per person. Subscribe to the online newsletter, *What's Cookin',* or call the store for class dates.

Bridger Kitchens and Culinary Center, 7540 Pioneer Way, Four Corners; (406) 582-1001; www.bridgerkitchens.com. Local chefs share their culinary secrets of the trade in these hands-on classes. The setting alone is worth the experience, given that this chichi design center spared no cost in the test kitchen (aka every cook's dream). Class themes range from country Italian to classic French sauces to the cuisines of Mexico, India, and Thailand. All classes include a light meal, wine, and nonalcoholic beverages. Classes start at 6:30 p.m. and cost $50–65 per person.

Brewpubs & Microbreweries

Bozeman Brewing Company, 504 North Broadway, Bozeman; (406) 585-9142; www.bozemanbrewing.com. Tapping the Bozeman locals' nickname for their town, owner and master brewer Todd Scott christened his brews "Bozone," as in Bozone Select Amber Ale, Bozone Hefe Weizen, and Bozone Plum Street Porter. Like so many others, Todd began his brewing career at home. He took it one step further, with an education from the venerable UC Davis program, and then he began brewing professionally for Napa Valley Brewing

Company in Calistoga, California. Later he moved back to Bozeman and brewed for Spanish Peaks for eleven years. And like the name Bozone, his beers and location in a cool industrial district have built a sense of community—to prove it, the local favorite brew, Hopzone IPA, won Best Montana Beer at the 2009 Montana Brew Fest. The taproom is in a historic building that was once a super-productive pea cannery that hit its height of production during World War II. Open Monday through Friday from 4 to 8 p.m. and Saturday from 12:30 to 8 p.m.

Lone Peak Brewery, 48 Market Place, Big Sky; (406) 446-4607; www.lonepeakbrewery.com. A true *micro*brewery, Lone Peak only produces 1,000 bottles per year. That may change as the beers grow in popularity. After only a year of production (the brewery opened in 2007), owners Steve and Vicky Nordahl could claim to be in every bar within the mountain hamlet of Big Sky.

The Lone Peak taproom is the best place to sample these beers, and they are generous with their samples—pouring a full pint of your choice. Named for the famous mountain that marks the pinnacle of the Big Sky and Moonlight Basin resorts, the beers—from the crisp, clean, and light Nordic Blonde to the Lone Peak IPA (pale ale) with its hoppy bitter-malty balance—are named with ski bum lingo in mind. Try the Headplant Pale Ale, Steep 'N Deep Winter Ale, or the Hippie Highway Oatmeal Stout and raise a pint in reverie any time of year. A casual restaurant serving burgers, brats, and nachos is blended with the taproom, open seven days a week from 11 a.m. to 8:30 p.m.

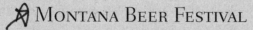 MONTANA BEER FESTIVAL

Reportedly the biggest brew fest from here to Portland, Oregon, the Montana Beer Festival boasts over 35 breweries, 200 beers, live music, and great food. This is not just a beer and brats kind of thing; these folks are serious about the beer brewing renaissance and the emergence of Rocky Mountain breweries. They bust out the stinky cheese for a pairing with choice locally crafted beers—who knew that creamy Gorgonzola could complement the flavors of a stout or that a grilled Thai beef stick would enhance the flavors in the Flathead Lake Rising Sun Espresso Porter. Sound good? Don't miss this seriously fun epicurean gathering. The event is held in early April, from 6 p.m. to midnight at the Gallatin County Fair Grounds in Bozeman.

> **Montana Beer Festival**
> **(406) 586-3426**
> **www.montanabeerfest.com**

 Madison River Brewing Company, 20900 Frontage Rd., Building B, Belgrade; (406) 388-0322; www.madisonriverbrewing.com. This is the home of "fly beers," all named after hand-tied bugs by fly-fishing fanatics in the taproom—you can order a Hopper, Yellow Humpy, Salmon Fly, Black Ghost, Copper John, Rubber Legged Razz, or the Irresistible. Not a surprise from a brewery named for the famous trout-rich river nearby. Look for the Salmon Fly Honey Rye, Hopper Pale Ale, Irresistible Amber Ale, and Copper John Scotch

Ale in restaurants and markets in Belgrade, Big Sky, Bozeman, Livingston, and Ennis. Owner Howard McMurray and master brewer Doug Frey also produce beer for three other companies—Big Hole Brewing, a Montana company famous for its Headstrong brand, and two Utah breweries, the Moab Brewery and Park City Brewing. The tasting room is located just on the edge of town and is open Tuesday through Saturday 2 p.m. to 8 p.m. Tours are available.

Montana Ale Works, 611 East Main St., Bozeman; (406) 587-7700; www.montanaaleworks.com. Centered on great Northwestern regional brews, the beer menu is the highlight of Ale Works' offerings. Seven signature drafts are created for the restaurant by Blackfoot River Brewing in Helena, Montana. Additionally there is a herd of Montana microbrews from breweries that dot the state from Missoula to Belt that you can sample until the cows come home. On top of that, the forty-tap selection is rounded out with quality pints from around the world. This is a beer lover's place, but it's certainly not limited to brews. The wine and spirits selection is tempting as well, and the menu, which they've dubbed "upscale comfort food," is varied enough that many visits to the popular hangout will not leave you bored. Food served here is fresh, local, and sustainable whenever possible. Ale Works serves natural local beef and bison (try the buffalo pot stickers with mango sauce or anything from the killer burger list). Also hard to resist are the Fish 'n' Chips (paired with a hearty brew, could there be any better combination?) and the Asian Noodle Salad with Tofu, if you are hanging out with a vegetarian.

More than a brewery, Ale Works is Bozeman's ultimate see-and-be-seen location. The menu is as extensive as the 8,000 square feet of grill, bar, and billiards area. And like today, the historic building has seen a century of action. Originally a warehouse owned by the Northern Pacific Railroad, the Ale Works gang has restored it, revitalized the east end of Main Street, and turned a funky old building into a place with enough character to appeal to families, foodies, and good friends any night of the week.

Neptune's Brewery, 119 North L St., Livingston; (406) 222-7837; www.neptunesbrewery.com. Although born and raised in Montana, owner and brewer Bill Taylor has a fascination with the sea. The wall-sized tropical aquarium that divides the taproom from the brewery is the first clue. Lest you think he's a little misguided for naming his brewery after the ruler of the seas and rivers when he is smack in the middle of dry land, Taylor reminds us on his Web site and in many conversations with his beer-loving friends that the Romans worshiped Neptune primarily as a horse god, Neptune Equester, patron of horse racing. By that definition, Taylor reasons that there is no better place to have a brewery than Montana, with its wild horses and clean mountain streams. Welcome to Neptune's Brewery. All-natural handcrafted beer. Brewed in the heart of Montana's Rocky Mountains. Beers include Neptune's Brewery Pale Ale, Smooth Sailing Cream Ale, Toad

Back Bock, Clipper Nut Brown Ale, and seasonal beers: Whale Tale Abbey, Chocolate Cream Porter, Shark Bite IPA, Dragging Anchor Lager, Oktoberfest Lager, Walk the Plank Stout. You'll find selections of Neptune's in Montana grocery stores and in Yellowstone National Park stores. Brewer Bill will give you a tour of the taproom, open daily from 4 to 8 p.m.

Red Lodge Ales, 1445 North Broadway, Red Lodge; (406) 446-4607; www.redlodgeales.com. This is arguably Montana's (and possibly the entire Rocky Mountains') greenest brewery. Owner and brewer Sam Hoffman is more conscientious than most about the sustainability of his operation. For starters, he uses only Montana-grown barley; his 12,000-square-foot brewery has the largest solar thermal array in the state of Montana. He uses hot water to heat the brewery in the winter and to heat-process water in the summer. In the winter months a refrigerator system exchanges air from the outside to save electricity by not using a conventional refrigeration system.

But the bottom line is that Sam makes good beer. The Hefeweizen, Porter, Jack's 90 Schilling Scottish Ale, Czechmate Pilsner, Bent Nail IPA, and Reserve Ale can vouch for that with a broad array and balance of flavors. It's the Beartooth Pale Ale that has proven a perennial favorite since Hoffman began brewing in Red Lodge in 1998. Look for Hoffman's beers in Red Lodge, Billings, Bozeman, Livingston, Helena, Missoula, the Flathead area, and Wyoming. The totally solar taproom is open every day from 2 to 8 p.m. during the summer, and 4 to 8 p.m. during the winter.

Dining Out in Yellowstone National Park

From cowboy to contemporary, historic lodges offer unique culinary experiences. Though the historic lodges of Yellowstone National Park (and their dining rooms) are technically in Wyoming, no visit to Montana is complete without a trip to the world's first national park. Here are some brief descriptions of the landmark eateries within Yellowstone's borders.

Yellowstone National Park Lodges concessionaire Xanterra Parks & Resorts Xanterra executive chef, Jim Chapman, lauds the company's overall focus on sustainable practices, including an initiative to buy 50 percent of food products from local, organic, all-natural, and sustainable sources by 2015. In 2008, the Yellowstone restaurants averaged over 30 percent, including food, wine, and beer. Xanterra's restaurants serve over one million diners each year. On the menus are natural Montana Ranch Brand beef burgers from Billings, fresh seafood from Bozeman's Montana Fish Company, and top-selling cuts of lamb from Wolf Ridge Lamb and Wool Company in Paradise Valley. Look for the "green earth logo" to special order these. To make reservations (where accepted) for all dining rooms in the park, call 1-866-GEYSERLAND (1-866-439-7375); www.travelyellowstone.net.

Canyon Lodge Dining Room; $$$. After the halting views of the Grand Canyon of the Yellowstone, head in to Canyon Lodge for its engaging offerings for breakfast, lunch, or dinner. On the dinner menu, items from the Northern Rockies region pepper the entree list.

Look for bison pot roast, sautéed Idaho trout, or the house specialty: prime rib. Open May through September.

Cowboy Cuisine, Lake Hotel; $$$. From Roosevelt Lodge, you can book a classic Old West chuck wagon dinner, complete with all-you-can-eat steak, corn muffins, "Rosi beans," potatoes, vegetable, and a fruit cobbler. Call to make arrangements for the ride and dinner. Available June through September.

Grant Village Dining Room, Grant Village; $$$. The dining room offers a breakfast buffet and specialty sandwiches and salads for lunch. Dinner is a sophisticated menu with something for everyone in this elegant, contemporary setting. (Reservations required for dinner.) Open May through September.

Lake Hotel Dining Room, Lake Hotel; $$$. History and elegance collide in this early 1900s structure. The menu is upscale and features farm-raised bison, wild Alaska salmon, and Montana Legend tenderloin with some stunning views of Yellowstone Lake. Breakfast, lunch, and dinner are served; reservations necessary. Open May through October.

Lake House Restaurant at Grant Village, Grant Village; $$$. At the Lake House on Yellowstone Lake meals are served with tremendous tableside views. A breakfast buffet and

continued on next page

casual dinners in a family-friendly atmosphere make this rustic lodge seem homey. Open May through September.

Mammoth Hot Springs Hotel, Lake Hotel; $$$. Views of what was once Fort Yellowstone from the dining room are intriguing. Open early May through early October; also December through March.

Old Faithful Inn, Lake Hotel; $$$. The Old Faithful is the most iconic dining room of Yellowstone, with its high-timbered ceilings and massive stone fireplace in a historic log building. Reservations are a must for dinner. Open May through October.

Old Faithful Snow Lodge Dining Room, Lake Hotel; $$$. The most contemporary of all the fine dining options in the park, Snow Lodge carries a distinctive wildlife motif throughout its design, offering a variety of food service styles in a captivating Western lodge environment. The menu features braised bison short ribs and wild Alaska salmon. The restaurant serves breakfast, lunch, and dinner. Open May through October; also December through March.

Roosevelt Dining Room, Lake Hotel; $$. Named for President Teddy Roosevelt, this dining room has an authentic rustic flavor. With columns made of large cedar logs and a roaring fire in the stone hearth, it's comfortably Western. The menu is a hearty list of entrees, including Rocky Mountain trout, bison sirloin, and surprisingly delicious fried chicken. The Lodge offers breakfast, lunch, and dinner. Reservations are not accepted. Open June through September.

Wolf Pack Brewing Company, 139 North Canyon St., West Yellowstone; (406) 646-7225. With a host of national-award-winning brews, Wolf Pack Brewing Company is known for its traditional German-style lagers. "Traditional" means they stand by the German law of purity—the Reinheitsgebot of 1516. You can have dinner here after your adventure in Yellowstone National Park. In honor of Yellowstone's famous wolves, try the Druid Pack Dunkleweizen, which won the gold medal in 2005 at the North American Beer Festival.

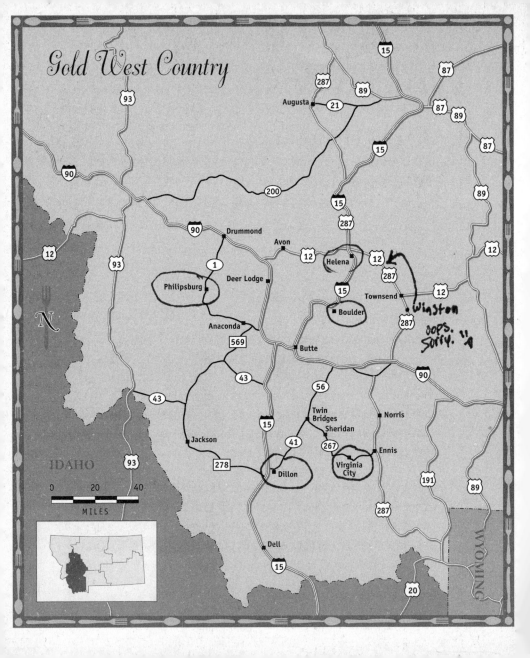

Gold West Country (West)

Grounded by Helena (the state capital) and Butte, this is a country full of pioneer dreams and deep history. The greatest concentrations of gold mines and ghost towns are in this part of the state. First came the Homestead Act of 1862, then the gold rush of 1863 to bring the first wave of pioneers, then, by the time the transcontinental railroad came through, from 1869 to the 1880s, gold country Montana was booming.

Communities popped up seemingly overnight as a result, including the great town of Butte, once home to the largest copper mines in the world. The mines brought thousands of immigrants from Europe and Asia, leaving behind a wonderful stew of ethnicity. The exceptional historic architecture speaks even now of the wealth and sophistication that existed here in the area's heyday. The "richest hill on earth," as it was called, in reference to the amount of copper mined here, was once the biggest city west of the Mississippi. Ornate mansions top the hilly streets above the boroughs of immigrant miners, who surged west from the 1870s through the 1950s, when the mine became less productive. Even now, standout restaurants punctuate the eclectic excellence that lives on here, reminders of Italian, Chinese, Eastern European, and Irish heritage.

Today, most of the gold and copper mining has dwindled; boom and bust cycles have left their mark. But what remains is glorious wheat and barley country in rolling farmland on the foothills of the Continental Divide. It's cattle country, too, with small towns peppering ranch pastures. From open prairie to valleys rimmed with mountains, the geographical diversity extends to the people and gives the region great personality and, therefore, pockets of good food.

Made or Grown Here

La Cense Beef, 4600 Carrigan Ln., Dillon; (866) 442-2333; www .lacensebeef.com. Every ranch will tell you that their beef tastes better. But La Cense free-range grass-fed beef honestly has a distinct flavor that sets it apart. I credit the fact that it is dry aged for nineteen days to round out its flavor and enhance its tenderness before it is hand cut and trimmed with care by skilled artisan butchers. It's also the focus on natural ranching that makes this beef exceptional. La Cense, owned by William Kriegel, is an 88,000-acre Black Angus and

La Cense Beef Steakhouse-Style Bone-In Tenderloin Filet

Steak houses serve steak like it should be, almost charred on the outside and almost rare on the inside. I have tried to re-create the magic on my small stove and have found that preheating my broiler for 15 minutes before putting the steaks under the flame works wonders. Another tip is to only use thick steaks; this will ensure that the heat from the broiler will not overcook the steak. La Cense has just introduced a twelve-ounce bone-in tenderloin filet and it is perfect for broiling in this manner. Recipe by Ulla Kjarval.

2 12-ounce La Cense Bone-In Tenderloin Filets
Salt and pepper to taste
Olive oil to cover steak

1. Salt and pepper the steaks and rub with a bit of olive oil. You want to bring the steaks to room temperature, so let them sit for half an hour before you broil them.
2. Preheat the broiler for 15 minutes. Broil the steaks for about 5 minutes on each side, but broilers vary greatly, so use your discretion. Accompany the steaks with creamed spinach and oven-fried potatoes.

Serves 2.

La Cense Beef
4600 Carrigan Ln., Dillon
(866) 442-2333
www.lacensebeef.com

✦ The Butte Pasty

Old-timers claim the pasty (pass-tee) arrived in Butte, Montana, along with the first housewives who followed their husbands into the mining camps. Long favored in the copper miner's lunch bucket, the pastry-wrapped meal was an ideal way for "Cousin Jeannie" to provide a hearty meal for the hard-working "Cousin Jack." As the miner unwrapped his lunch, he would refer to the pasty as a "letter from 'ome." Its popularity spread quickly throughout the camp, and today the pasty is as much a part of Butte as the Berkeley Pit. Recipe from Montana Celebrity Cookbook by Susie Beaulaurier Graetz.

Pastry

3 cups flour

1 teaspoon salt

1 ¼ cups lard or shortening

¾ cup very cold water

Filling

5 or 6 medium potatoes (red are best), sliced

3 medium or 2 large yellow onions, diced

1 tablespoon parsley to taste

2 pounds of meat (loin tip, skirting, or flank steak), thinly sliced

½ cup (1 stick) cold butter, cubed

Salt and pepper to taste

Milk for brushing

horse ranch. Its beef is only available straight from the ranch, where it is frozen and vacuum-packed at the time of processing (at a USDA-certified plant) to ensure that you receive the highest quality beef at your doorstep. All orders can be shipped overnight or two-day air.

Pastry

1. Preheat oven to 375°F.
2. Measure flour and salt. Cut in lard until dough resembles small peas.
3. Add water and divide into 6 equal parts.
4. Roll individual pieces of dough into slightly oblong shapes.

Filling

1. Layer filling ingredients on dough, first the potatoes, onions, meat.
2. Top each filling with 6-8 cubes of butter, sprinkle with parsley, salt, and pepper to taste.
3. Bring pastry dough up from ends and crimp across the top. Making the pasty oblong eliminates the lump of dough on each end.
4. Brush a little milk on top and bake at 375°F for about one hour until golden brown.

Serves 6.

Montana City Sauces, 1 Jackson Creek Rd., Montana City; (406) 933-5440; www.montanacitygrill.com. From the kitchen of the notable Montana City Grill, near Helena, comes a line of sauces that are classic features of the restaurant's vast menu. Developed at the restaurant

GRASS IS GOOD

Grass-fed beef is good for cows, good for preserving land, and good for people. It's just that simple. For a list of Montana ranches that raise livestock—from bison to lamb—with grass-fed principles, go to www.eatwild.com.

since 1998, original recipes for Gourmet Red BBQ and Huckleberry BBQ sauces, London Broil, Spicy Oriental, and Southwest Dippin' Sauce have been bottled for cooking at home. These sauces are available from the Web site and at regional specialty food stores.

Vigilante Distilling, (406) 465-1215; www.vigilantedistilling .com. Mike Uda, a lawyer by trade, saw an opportunity develop when a new state law passed, making it legal for a "microdistillery" to produce hard alcohol in Montana. Now Helena's first distillery produces vodka and gin, and it plans eventually to also produce fine whiskey and other handcrafted alcohols. Look for Vigilante products in liquor stores around Helena.

Wild Echo Bison Ranch, P.O. Box 890, Townsend; (406) 202-2377; www.wildechobison.com. Although Wild Echo's bison meat is sold at Helena's Real Food Market, this is not your typical meat supplier. Pam and Craig Knowles raise around fifty head of bison at the ranch, on 480 acres in the Big Belt Mountains southeast of Townsend. They started in 1995, before bison meat was "cool" to eat, and they now sell mostly in Helena or directly to clients. These bison are treated like pets in a way; they are named and cared for

THE DINING CAR

From murder mysteries to wildlife watching, the Copper King Express keeps the dining car lively on these annual adventures. For close to one hundred years, the Butte, Anaconda & Pacific (B.A.&P.). Railway provided the Anaconda smelter and copper mines cost-effective railroad transportation—seven days a week, around the clock. It was commonly referred to as "The Biggest Little Railroad in the World." Around 1912, it was moving about 30,000 tons per day, or about 600 carloads. The railroad closed in the 1980s and was later revived by a private company, featuring restored vintage 1951 train cars for public railway travel. Traveling from Anaconda to Butte and back, the trip lasts approximately three hours. Today, passenger service (and dinner!) is available on the Copper King Express. For reservations, (877) 563-5458; www.copperkingexpress.com.

and kept healthy on all-natural grasses and hay. Wild Echo also offers a "green" bison luxury camping experience that has been featured on ABC's *20/20*, a Sundance Channel series, and MSNBC.

Specialty Stores & Markets

Asia West Mart, 222 North Main St., Deer Lodge; (406) 846-1282. Tired of driving to Seattle or paying online shipping fees for the ingredients for chicken adobo or *lumpia*, Elvie Wells decided to open her own Asian specialty food shop in 2009. Set up in the clean,

Elvie's Asian-Glazed Chicken Thighs

8 chicken thighs

Marinade
Finely grated zest of 2 oranges
¾ cup fresh orange juice
¼ cup honey
2 tablespoons toasted sesame
  oil
1 tablespoon minced fresh
  ginger

1 tablespoon minced garlic
¼ teaspoon crushed red pepper
  flakes
3 tablespoons soy sauce
Salt and pepper to taste
8 ounces rice noodles
4 scallions, thinly sliced, for
  garnish

Marinade

1. The day before serving, rinse the chicken and pat dry. Place in a
   bowl.
2. Combine the orange zest, orange juice, honey, sesame oil, ginger,
   garlic, red pepper flakes, and soy sauce to make a marinade; toss
   with chicken to coat. Cover the chicken and refrigerate for 4 to 6
   hours, or overnight.

enclosed front porch of her home, across from the local fairgrounds,
Asia West is in the least likely place you'd imagine finding Thai,
Japanese, Filipino, and Chinese food items and accessories. But

Chicken

1. Thirty minutes before cooking, remove chicken from the refrigerator. Preheat the oven to 350°F.
2. Arrange the chicken in a large, shallow roasting pan and season with salt and pepper to taste. Pour the marinade over the chicken.
3. Bake the chicken, basting frequently, until golden brown and cooked through, about 45 minutes.
4. Meanwhile, bring a large pot of water to boil. Turn off the heat and stir in rice noodles. Let soak until tender, about 7 minutes. Drain, rinse, and drain again.
5. Divide the noodles between four bowls. Place 2 chicken thighs in each bowl and spoon the pan sauce over the top. Garnish with the scallions and serve immediately.

Serves 6–8.

step through the door and be pleasantly surprised by the selection of hard-to-find ingredients for your favorite Asian cuisine. Elvie also sells premade frozen meals that can be reheated in your oven. Be

Food with History:
Don't Pass on the Pasty

A hearty tradition brought from Cornwall, England, and packed in the lunch boxes of Butte's hard-working miners, the pasty is a blue-collar culinary item that lives on today.

Joe's Pasty Shop, 1641 Grand Ave., Butte; (406) 723-9071; $. This is the most famous of them all, according to owner Tom Laity, who says "People from Cornwall say our pasties taste the same as the ones at home."

Nancy McLaughlin's Pasty Shop, 2810 Pine St., Butte; (406) 782-7410; $. This shop serves up an elegant version of the carry-out dish, topped with gravy. The thirty-year-old shop near the Berkeley Pit—the city's abandoned mile-wide copper mine—also serves a mean pork chop sandwich.

Park Street Pasties, 800 West Park St., Butte; (406) 782-6400; $. The newcomer on the block (since 2002), Park Street makes homemade pasties that feature cut-up steak, potatoes, and onions and have become local sweethearts.

Town Talk Bakery, 611 East Front St., Butte; (406) 782-4985; $. Forty years after it opened in 1936, the bakery was a wedding present from William Spear Sr. to his son, William Spear Jr. This shop is known for Italian breadsticks, Finnish health bread, and pasties filled with ground sirloin.

Wind's Bakery and Pasty Shop, 208 East Park Ave., Anaconda; (406) 563-2362; $. Since 1990 Mike Austin (who worked here as a teenager) and his wife, Bobbi, have made these well-known (after fifty years, they should be!) favorites available in grocery stores throughout the state.

sure to take a cooler and buy a pack of spring rolls (*lumpia*). They're so good that they're worth driving 150 miles to stock up; the filling (made of pork and vegetables) is close to the texture of pâté and the wrapper is thinner than paper.

Booze & Buns, 108 Main St., Sheridan; (406) 842-5790. Like so many places in Montana, this little business wears many hats—it is one part liquor store, one part specialty wine shop, one part gourmet bakery. That explains the name, but it shouldn't be a deterrent. In the town of Sheridan (population 700), the shop is a great resource for good things. Located in the former Masonic Hall, Booze & Buns serves up fresh pastries and coffee worth stopping for on the way into the Ruby River Valley.

The Copper Kettle Chocolates and Gem Gallery, 2000 Harrison Ave., Butte; (406) 723-4044; www.copperkettlechocolates. com. Owner Coleen Le Fever has reclaimed this little restored 1906 home and specializes in handmade chocolates, twenty-one flavors of fudge, truffles, taffy, and . . . jewelry (not edible). This funky little shop tries hard and makes some good candy.

Doe Brother's Restaurant and Old Fashioned Soda Fountain, 120 East Broadway, Philipsburg; (406) 859-7677; www. doebrothers.net. With the slogan "Any time is ice cream time," owners Ruth Ann and Tony Marchi are my kind of folks. They relocated and remodeled this historic malt shop and now joke that they are glorified busboys, but in truth, their willingness to work all aspects of this restaurant make them torchbearers to history. The well-worn marble counter at this 1887 soda fountain shows the marks of much use: It was put in place by M. E. Doe and his brother-in-law J. D. Thomas in one of Philipsburg's oldest buildings. The conversations and stories shared by customers here over more than a century make this a special spot—not to mention the scrumptious sundaes and old-style sodas. If dessert-first is not your mantra, on the restaurant side they serve immense sandwiches—the Philly (as in Philipsburg, not Philadelphia) Cheesesteak is worth the caloric splurge—along with soups and salads.

Firetower Coffee, 422 North Last Chance Gulch, Helena; (406) 495-8840; www.firetowercoffee.com. Serving coffees and teas in a very cozy atmosphere, Firetower is a great place to linger in a comfy armchair, but you can also continue your stroll along Last Chance Gulch. Incredible breakfast sandwiches and even better panini keep this coffee shop hoppin'.

Front Street Market, 8 West Front St., Butte; (406) 782-2614. The advice friends offer when they hear of a visit to this specialty market is this: Bring your cooler. Front Street Market is a little out of the way (unless you live in Butte), but it is sure to have hard-to-find food items that you'll want to lug home. This market and deli carries the state's widest selection of Italian food specialties (I always stock up on ladyfingers for tiramisu; Butte's the only place within 150 miles that sells them) but also items from France, Germany, Greece, Japan, and Mexico. You'll want to take home the

A CAPITOL RIDE

Great Northern Carousel, 924 Bicentennial Plaza, Great Northern Town Center in historic downtown Helena; (406) 457-5353; www.gncarousel.com. When the West was won, who knew that meant riding astride trout, bison, bears, and even dinosaurs? At the charming Great Northern Carousel, all that is possible. The enclosed pavilion features hand-sculptured chariots and thirty-eight animals that reawaken the whimsy of childhood for everyone. The carousel is decorated with stained-glass murals of the

Capitol, the fire tower, the civic center, elk, and grizzly bears, made by Helena artist Mary Harris. The west-facing windows of the building are original stained glass from the century-old remains of the Old Broadwater Hotel of Helena.

The nostalgic Painted Pony Ice Cream Parlor is the cherry on top of a visit to the carousel, serving sundaes, ice cream cones, and lunch.

housemade ravioli and countless other goodies for your own freezer. Not too long ago, Jim and Marla Yakawich expanded the wine selection, now offering 2,000 different choices from all over the world. Gourmet cheeses, salami, and other cured delectables are found in the deli, along with shelves stocked from floor to ceiling with so many items you'll find it pleasantly overwhelming.

While you're here, you can fortify yourself for more menu planning or the long drive home with lunch at the deli: housemade soups, salads, and sandwiches. Have a seat outside in summer months or inside, amongst the shelves of food, at any of the green-and-white-striped tables. It's worth the drive just for lunch, but even more so to immerse yourself in foodieland for the afternoon.

Painted Pony Ice Cream Parlor, 924 Bicentennial Plaza, Helena; (406) 457-5353; www.gncarousel.com. Inside the Great Northern Carousel pavilion, the Painted Pony Ice Cream Parlor serves up locally made ice cream from Great Northern Ice Cream Company. Choose from twenty-four flavors, including an ever-changing flavor of the month, plus seasonal favorites like apple, watermelon, cantaloupe, and peach. But it's the regular flavors on the menu that are irresistible: Try Carousel Cotton Candy, Grizzly Grub Huckleberry, or Flathead Cherry.

The Pan Handler, 40 South Last Chance Gulch, Helena; (406) 443-1916. Owner Billie Shepard opened this store in 1979, before gourmet cooking at home was a common pastime. Her store in historic Helena has grown with the times, featuring high-end cookery and specialty food products from Montana and beyond.

Park Avenue Bakery & Café, 44 South Park Ave., Helena; (406) 449-8424. Old-world charm lives on at this European-style bakery in historic Helena. Situated in the old Eddy's Bakery building, the bakery offers artisanal breads and pastries daily. The chicken potpie is a hearty favorite for lunch—perfect for a cool autumn day.

Parrot Confectionery Store, 42 North Main St., Helena; (406) 442-1470. Iconic and nostalgic, the Parrot is a Helena landmark for its wondrous selection of candy and back-in-time ambiance. It has changed little since opening in 1922 as a neighborhood soda fountain. Today, the wooden booths and checkered floors are antique, but the delicious sundaes are fresh and the chocolates made here are "the best ever," as longtime customers will tell you. Parrot makes 120 different candies and chocolates, but before you splurge, try the homemade chili. Yes, chili. Those in the know swear by it and beg Dave Duensing for the recipe to no avail. My guess is that they spice it with the slightest bit of unsweetened cocoa.

Real Food Market & Deli, 1096 Helena Ave., Helena; (406) 443-5150; www.realfoodstore.com. Since 1975 this market has promoted healthy living through fresh, local, and organic foods. Real Food is arguably Montana's first organic food store, and the idea of eating well and living well is pervasive here. Supporting local farmers and ranchers, the store offers thousands of food items and resources for alternative medicine. The deli serves up great sandwiches made to order and a hot daily menu (chicken cordon bleu for this writer, thank you very much).

Sweetgrass Bakery, 322 Fuller Ave., Helena; (406) 443-1103. This bakeshop uses organic and locally grown ingredients and grinds its own Montana grains on site. You'll be surprised at the difference in bread's texture when it's made with freshly ground flour. From Scottish oatmeal loaves to challah, the bread here is something this writer craves. Add to that other tempting items like the whole wheat cinnamon rolls, five varieties of Danish, and brioche, and I'll confess that this is my must-stop place every time I am in town. Sweetgrass has been a Helena staple since 1977.

The Sweet Palace, 109 East Broadway, Philipsburg; (888) SWEET-XO (793-3896) or (406) 859-3353; www.sweetpalace .com. Can you list your top ten favorite candies? At the Sweet Palace, you may be muddled with the conundrum of hundreds of choices. Owner Shirley Beck says the Red Licorice Wheels, Sugar Plums gels, Sour Lemon Napoleons, Dark Chocolate Moose Drool Premium Truffles, and Mint Humbugs are the best sellers. At this dreamy confectionary, you can watch how enchanting Victorian-era candy is made. Open since 1998, this sweet spot has become legendary in the historic mining town. Choose from any of fifty kinds of fudge, seventy-two flavors of saltwater taffy, twenty varieties of caramels, and don't miss the treat of sampling the numerous chocolates. The shop is closed on Saturdays, but don't despair; you can order from the online catalog.

Toppers Cellar and Spirits, 1221 Helena Ave., Helena; (406) 442-9357. A little out of the way, but worth the crosstown search,

Toppers is known for its incredible beer and wine selection, as well as interesting spirits. The staff is knowledgeable and the choices are extensive.

Virginia City Creamery, 205 West Wallace St., Virginia City; (406) 843-5513. Using a recipe from an old White House cookbook, the Creamery churns up real homemade ice cream. People watch ice cream being made in an antique ice cream freezer with an old hit-or-miss engine providing the power to turn the machine. It's part of Virginia City's historic pioneer presentation, and on a "hit" day during open season (May through September), nothing beats a scoop of *real* vanilla.

Yesterday's Soda Fountain, 124 Main St., Ennis; (406) 682-4246. Walk into Yesterday's, where a pink marble soda fountain and a back bar that were originally installed in Blakesley's Cigar Store in Forsyth, Montana, circa 1929 bring back a sense of nostalgia. Sidle up to a classic swivel stool and enjoy the simplicity of a sundae with all the toppings. Established in 1994, Yesterday's is located in the 1905 Ennis Pharmacy building, the oldest building giving continuous service to the Madison Valley. More than just a bit of nostalgia, this place is a gathering spot for locals and families who enjoy the sweet treats—old-fashioned sodas and newfangled smoothies, right alongside the usual delicious ice cream dishes.

Boulder Farmer's Market, Veteran's Park on Main St., Boulder. Saturday from 9 a.m. to noon, June through September.

Bullwhacker Block Saturday Market, Historic Walking Mall between 6th Ave. and Broadway, on the Bullwhacker Block, Helena. Saturday 8 a.m. to 1 p.m., April through late August.

Butte Farmers' Market, Park and Main Streets, Uptown Butte. Saturday 9 a.m. to 1 p.m., May through October.

Deer Lodge Sunday Farmers Market, 500 block of Main St., Deer Lodge. Sunday 8 a.m. to 1 p.m., July through October

Dillon Farmers' Market, Wells Fargo Bank parking lot, Dillon. Saturday 9 a.m. to noon, July through September.

Helena Farmer's Market, between Neil and West Placer on Fuller Ave., Helena. Saturday 9 a.m. to 1 p.m., April through November. Also held on Wednesdays at varying locations as part of the community's Alive @ 5 series, which organizes music, art, and markets each week. Four p.m. to 6:30 p.m., July through September. Check www.downtownhelena.com for locations.

Madison Farm to Fork Farmers Market, lawn of the First Madison Valley Bank, Financial Center, on Highway 287, 2 miles north of Ennis. Saturday 9 a.m. to noon, late May through September.

Virginia City Artisans and Growers Guild, downtown Virginia City. Saturday 9 a.m. to noon, June through September. The one-room log schoolhouse in historic Virginia City, built in 1873, is now used as a gift shop and hosts a farmers' market.

Whitehall Farmer's Market, City Park, Whitehall. Saturday 9 a.m. to noon, June through September.

Food Happenings

MARCH

St. Patrick's Day, Butte; www.butteamerica.com. One of the largest Saint Paddy's celebrations outside of Boston, 30,000 people assemble for the March 17th parade, but also tag on two more days of corned beef and cabbage feasting and other gatherings. The St. Patrick's Day Parade lines up and leaves from Mercury Street and continues through the historic Uptown District to enjoy the parade led by the Ancient Order of Hibernians and celebrate in bars such as Maloney's, the Silver Dollar Saloon, the M&M Cigar Store, and The Irish Times Pub where booths made from church pews imported from

Dublin ensconce revelers. A stone at the main door imported from County Clare allows visitors to literally touch Irish soil (or stone to be exact) as they enter the pub.

MAY

Brewery Follies, Virginia City; (800) 829-2969; www.virginiacity .com. Dinner theater at its bawdiest: The Brewery Follies launch their summer season review with old-time vaudevillian acts with a contemporary twist. Watch with a smile and a libation in Montana's first brewery, the H. S. Gilbert Brewery, and enjoy a performance.

Historic Virginia City is a tourist destination that also draws many locals. The Gilbert Brewery building hosts The Brewery Follies, and the zany theatrics of this professional troupe begin on Memorial Day and continue through Labor Day. There are two shows daily (4 and 8 p.m.). Call (406) 843-5218 for reservations.

In celebration of the building's original use (when Virginia City was the gold rush capital of the Rocky Mountains), the Follies serve up Missoula-brewed Bayern beers, along with other Montana micro-brews on tap. The local favorite, Moose Drool, is a tasty nut-brown ale brewed by Missoula's Big Sky Brewing Company. Gilbert's Beer from Lewis and Clark Brewery in Helena is another likable option.

Firemen's Clam Bake, Philipsburg. In support of the hardworking volunteer firefighters of Phillipsburg, the community ventures out to the annual clam bake at the town hall. The fund-raiser for the fire department is the unofficial spring fling, as the snow finally melts off in the mountains and townsfolk emerge to share a celebratory meal for a good cause. For tickets, call the local Town Hall for more information (406-859-3821); or the Philipsburg Chamber of Commerce (406-859-3388).

JULY

Dog & Grog Montana Microbrew Festival, Virginia City; 344 West Wallace St.; (406) 843-5700. Montana loves its dogs and beer . . . hence the name. It's nothing more than that. The barbecue is held on the patio of the Bale of Hay Saloon in historic Virginia City. Saturday showcases the best Montana breweries, with ten breweries and more than twenty-five brews on tap from noon to 7 p.m.

Heritage Days & Victorian Ball, Virginia City; (406) 843-5700; www.virginiacity.com. History buffs come to life at this annual foot-stompin' event and step back in time. It's a celebration of the Victorian era with a Grand Ball where guests attend in period costume. To start off the ball, tea is served in the style of the early 1900s and instructors offer lessons on customs and the dances.

AUGUST

Art & Jazz on Broadway, Philipsburg; (406) 859-7799 or (406) 859-0066; www.artinphilipsburg.com. Original art and lively jazz come to historic downtown Philipsburg. This annual event showcases the works of painters, potters, weavers, woodworkers, and sculptors. Crowds are entertained with live jazz while sipping microbrews, sampling wines, and tasting cheese. The main street closes to traffic and tables are set up along the length of town for diners to enjoy outdoor meals from 11 a.m. to 5 p.m.

OCTOBER

Hunters Feed and Wild Game Cook-Off, Ennis; (406) 682-4388. Each year on the Friday before hunting season begins, Main Street of Ennis hosts a feast. Local businesses prepare wild game dishes using elk, venison, antelope, pheasant, duck, and grouse. The public samples and votes on the tastiest preparation. Dishes such as wild pheasant with dill sauce, deer fudge, moose meatballs, and elk chili delight diners. The fun begins at 3 p.m.; come hungry.

Oktoberfest, Anaconda; 401 East Commercial Ave.; (406) 563-2422. The Copper Village Museum and Arts Center hosts an annual farmers' market and serves up traditional German fare—sausages, potato salad, kraut, hot rolls, and other wonderful food—accompanied by a beer garden. Music, crafts, and community are the attractions at this harvesttime gathering. The family fun event takes place in early October from 10 a.m. to 5 p.m.

DECEMBER

Breakfast with Santa, Helena; 15 Jackson St.; (406) 447-1535; www.downtownhelena.com. Hosted by the Shriners, this event offering pancakes, eggs, and seatings to see the merry old elf himself is a great way to raise money for children in need of medical assistance. Seatings at 9, 10, and 11 a.m. Reservations are a must.

Landmark Eateries

Avon Café, 13436 Highway 12 East, Avon; (406) 492-6381; $. Drive the back roads between Helena and Missoula, and you'll come across this old-timey rural restaurant. You might catch the local farmers and ranchers sitting around the table telling stories and solving the world's problems. Surrounded by rolling farmland, this cafe is located in one of Montana's smallest towns. As much a community center as a cafe, Avon serves breakfast all day and several kinds of fresh-baked pie. The cinnamon rolls are a favorite, as is the classic chicken-fried steak.

Barclay II Supper Club, 1300 East Commercial Ave., Anaconda; (406) 563-5541; $$. What this classic Western supper club lacks in glitzy atmosphere, it makes up for with authentic Montana hospitality. Family-owned and operated by three generations for over twenty years, this is a one-of-a-kind place. Prepare yourself to enjoy a full seven-course meal. Barclay II serves the classics—steak, chicken, seafood—and has been touted as serving the best steaks in all of Montana. You'll have to decide that on your own.

Benny's Bistro, 108 East 6th Ave., Helena; (406) 443-0105; www .bennysbistro.com; $$$. Travel to Delhi, Tunisia, Rio, or Tuscany through the theme dinners prepared at this locals' favorite. The chef prepares these special menus for large parties, but on a day-to-day basis you can find classic American bistro-style cuisine with an emphasis on fresh local ingredients. In Montana a good steak is easy to find, but creative dishes that feature locally-grown-veggie-filled crepes or savory smoked trout are more difficult. This is the place, just off Last Chance Gulch in historic downtown Helena.

Continental Divide, 47 Geyser St., Ennis; (406) 682-7600; $$$. This country bistro is a summer tradition in this fly-fishing mecca, though it's not just for fishermen. It's been written up in publications such as the *New York Times,* the *Washington Post, Esquire, Town & Country*, and *Gourmet*—not too shabby for a forty-seat restaurant with a dirt parking lot and a couple of hitching posts out front. Since 1982 the CD has been serving up creative American cuisine, with an emphasis on fresh ingredients, great steaks, and beautiful presentation. Dine al fresco with the gorgeous backdrop of the Madison Range from June through September. Try the elk medallions with porcini sauce or ask owner Eric Trapp to recommend the special that best incorporates fresh, regional ingredients.

Fetty's Bar & Café, Highway 43, Wisdom; (406) 689-3260; $. One of the few places where you can order Rocky Mountain oysters (fried bull testicles) right off the menu and where you might not regret it. Also one of the only restaurants in tiny Wisdom, this authentic cowboy cafe has been here since 1932, cooking for ranchers, farmers, and fishermen in the Big Hole Valley. More of them order the classic burgers or chicken-fried steak than the "oysters," and the homemade snickerdoodle cookies are easy to tuck into your pocket to snack on later.

Filling Station Creperie, 48 North Last Chance Gulch, Helena; (406) 459-6484; $. Francophiles gleefully speak French at this little eatery. There are three different types of batter for the crepes, and they are cooked on a French cast-iron crepe grill. Favorites include the four-berry crepe and the ham and cheese, but there's everything from lamb crepes with a side salad to a sweet apple crepe with mascarpone cheese called the Normandy. But you don't have to speak the language to eat the food!

Gamers Café, 15 West Park St., Butte; (406) 723-5453; $. Since 1904 this traditional Western luncheonette has been known for its chicken pies and Cornish pasties. The menu is what locals call "traditional miners' fare," as a tribute to Butte's past.

Jackson Hot Springs Lodge, Main St./Montana Highway 278, Jackson; (406) 834-3151; www.jacksonhotsprings.com; $$. Though the accommodations at this remote lodge are nothing fancy (cozy and rustic is more apt), the pool is natural and hot (and doesn't smell like hard-boiled eggs) and the food is elaborate. Surrounded by cabins, the lodge at the center is a gathering place, featuring a bar that centers on a massive fireplace. The restaurant is tucked in back, in a quiet, intimate setting. The meals in the lodge dining room, where the staff makes an effort to support local organic farmers and use their produce when possible, have become legendary. Some of the dishes on the menu will make your mouth water: hazelnut-and-herb-crusted pork chops; roasted portobello mushrooms layered with fresh spinach, tomato, and goat cheese, served with basil mashed potatoes, and drizzled with a port wine reduction; pan-fried trout amandine; marinated ostrich flank steak; and roasted pheasant with potato dumpling and a sour cream–mushroom sauce, to name just a few. But personally, I like to keep it simple: prime rib, medium rare. Pass the horseradish, please.

Last Chance Ranch, 2884 Grizzly Gulch, Helena; (800) 505-2884; www.lastchanceranch.biz; $$$$. Real western fun begins with a wagon ride up to Last Chance Ranch's Moose Meadow Tipi. That's where an evening of cowboy campfire music and an excellent meal await. Enjoy a great gourmet meal—meat and potatoes, Montana style. One price includes a shuttle from Helena to the ranch, the wagon ride, and dinner.

Lucca's, 56 North Last Chance Gulch, Helena; (406) 457-8311; www.luccasitalian.com; $$$. A landmark because it is not a steak house or a Western saloon (though you can order a nice New York strip steak and an excellent cocktail) in this Wild West town, Lucca's dishes out authentic Italian pastas in a clean-lined contemporary atmosphere. An extensive wine list leans to the pricier side, but the knowledgeable staff is helpful enough to make it a worthwhile purchase. Open nightly for dinner.

Mel's Diner, 121 Main St., Augusta; (406) 562-3408; $. Not like the Mel's Diner of the 70s TV show at all, this place is as much a community meeting hall as any place in little Augusta. Here, on the vast openness of the Rocky Mountain Front, the restaurant invites conversation and company, especially during the long, windy, and bitterly cold winter months. But at other times, it's a great place for a malt, made with Montana's own Wilcoxson's ice cream and sipped at one of the half-dozen booths. You'll likely need to slide up to share space with a friendly resident, since Mel's is usually packed with customers. The menu ranges from chili to burgers and is satisfying, but the company is generally better.

Norris Hot Springs, Highway 84 at Junction 287, Norris; (406) 685-3303; www.norrishotsprings.com; $. Eat. Drink. Soak. If that doesn't boil down the essentials of life, what does? At Norris, a roadside natural hot spring plunge with a whole lotta soul, those are the priorities. The No Loose Dogs Café and Saloon bills itself as a poolside snack bar, but, in fact, it's a food lover's delight with a spare menu focused on fresh, local, seasonal vegetables and food that just plain tastes good. The wine list is a refreshing surprise, as well, serving everything from Shiraz to Pinot Grigio. My recommendation on a hot summer day is a sip of cold, bubbly Prosecco before (and after) a dip in the pure geothermal pool.

The Old Hotel, 101 East 5th Ave., Twin Bridges; (406) 684-5959; www.theoldhotel.com; $$$. Catering mostly to fly fishermen because of its proximity to three blue-ribbon trout streams (Ruby, Big Hole, and Jefferson), this B&B restaurant also serves travelers who seek it out simply because of the excellent cuisine. This quaint eatery offers a prix fixe menu that changes weekly and gives diners a choice of two options each night. Incorporating local ingredients whenever possible, chef-owners Paula and Bill cook up a cuisine that uniquely blends Pacific Rim and European flavors—one night that means panko-crusted salmon and another it may be tandoori-grilled bison filets. The Old Hotel was built in 1879. After a 1996 renovation, the three-story brick building stands sentinel over the quiet little town of Twin Bridges. Open Thursday through Sunday; reservations strongly recommended.

Pekin Noodle Parlor, 117 South Main St., Butte; (406) 782-2217; $$. On the edge of Butte's historic Chinatown, at the one remaining Chinese noodle parlor in town, customers climb the steps to sit in pink booths and eat chow mein, chop suey, and other favorites from a menu that has not changed in thirty years. Because of its mining history, Butte's population in the early 1900s was one-third immigrants, a huge portion of whom were Chinese. The Pekin, with its neon CHOP SUEY sign out front, is a prime example of the Chinese-American experience. The authenticity of Butte's Chinese culture melding with American tradition resounds as loudly as the rattling dim sum cart that rolls up to your table in this dingy—but worthwhile—Butte establishment. Closed Tuesday.

Philipsburg Café, 127 East Broadway, Philipsburg; (406) 859-7799; www.thephilipsburgcafe.com; $$. Mike and Meredith Sauer opened this small-town restaurant in 2006 after their retreat from the East Coast rat race. Things are now idyllic for them in this Norman Rockwell–type town. A trained chef, Mike cooks up hearty breakfast and lunch daily and adds a spice of variety to a limited monthly dinner menu that ranges from prime rib to stuffed trout.

Pork Chop John's, 8 West Mercury St., Butte; (406) 782-0812; www.porkchopjohns.com; $. It's an acquired taste, some say, but in Butte the pork chop sandwich is a staple. In 1932 John Burklund introduced his sandwich—a thin-cut pork loin, lightly battered, deep-fried, and served on a bun with pickles, onions, and mus-tard—to the town, and diners have been pining for it ever since. Locals will tell you it's a must in Butte; you be the judge.

R-B Drive-in, 932 Helena Ave., Helena; (406) 442-7482; $. R-B stands for "root beer," which is still a popular beverage at this old-fashioned burger joint. On the same corner since 1938, the R-B Drive-In is a Helena institution. It's the kind of place that serves up a generous dose of nostalgia with the most-popular Double Bacon-Loaded Deluxe Cheeseburger and fries. Don't forget the special sauce—a mixture of mayonnaise, Tabasco, and ketchup. Oh, and a chocolate shake, blended just like in the old days.

Silver Star Steak Company, 833 Great Northern Blvd., Helena; (406) 495-0677; www.silverstarsteakco.com; $$$. Sloughing off the old idea of a supper club, Silver Star Steak Company steps out of the box with racy additions to the menu—case in point, the stuffed flatiron steak that is grilled and stuffed with blue cheese and red onion frills. Or Philly Cheesesteak Spring Rolls (yes, really): shaved rib-eye, mushrooms, and onions rolled in a spring roll wrapper, fried till crisp, and then topped with marinara and cheese sauce. And don't overlook what the gang here calls "Steak Enhancers": sautéed mushrooms, caramelized onions, bourbon peppercorn sauce, coffee rub, blackening spice, blue cheese mousse. The menu also features seafood and poultry dishes. Casual and fun for the after-work crowd or a family dinner, dressed up or dressed down, this is Montana, where the atmosphere is versatile and welcoming.

Sommeliers Wine Bar, 361 North Last Chance Gulch St., Helena; (406) 442-3685; www.sommelierswinebar.com. This wine boutique draws aficionados and novices alike into the culture of wine drinking. Sommeliers makes it easy with a list of wines by the glass that range from Champagne to reds and whites of interest. Monthly tastings and a wine club foster the spirit of sharing information. Guests can pair wines by the glass with a nice list of appetizer-size plates that range from a cheese board to baked Brie to hummus and bread. Wines by the bottle, along with all the accoutrements, such as glassware, corkscrews, and decanters, are also available.

Star Bakery Restaurant, 1576 U.S. Highway 287, Virginia City; (406) 843-5525; www.starbakeryrestaurant.com; $$. Touristy, but irresistible for the simple fact that it is in a log cabin, Star Bakery will surprise you with fantastic food. The original restaurant first opened in 1865, serving miners a fine loaf of bread, beer, and meals. Today the friendly crew serves sandwiches, soups, and salads. The Emporium side offers fudge, candy, and ice cream in a very cute historic setting.

Toi's Thai Cuisine, Helena, 423 North Last Chance Gulch St., Helena; (406) 443-6656; $$. Jamriang Toi Tyler offers authentic Thai cuisine. The menu includes favorites such as pad Thai, a tender chicken satay, the classic hot and sour soup, tom yum goong, and green and red curries. Loyal diners swear it is the best Thai food they've ever eaten. I wouldn't go that far, but it *is* excellent and I'm thankful for some "Thai hot" options in Montana. The restaurant is tiny. It opens at 5 p.m.; by 5:30 there are no tables left, so get there early.

Uptown Café, 47 East Broadway, Butte; (406) 723-4735; www .uptowncafe.com; $$. Influenced by French, Italian, and Cajun cuisine, the menu at the Uptown is varied and approachable. For two decades it's been a consistent favorite. Set in the heart of the historic uptown district, the restaurant offers convenient and quick cafe lunches and elegant dinners in the evenings. My favorite starter is the Clams Maison (baked in butter and herbs and served with bread). Some folks say it's the best restaurant in Montana, where the best of Butte tradition meets lively up-to-the-minute sauces and ingredients.

Eh.
Overrated!

Windbag Saloon & Eatery, 19 South Last Chance Gulch, Helena; (406) 443-9669; $$$. Established in 1978, this is still the first place locals recommend to eat in Helena. Located on the historic walking mall downtown, this classic steak house has capitalized on the town's gold mining history, with vintage photos and colorful stories of Wild West shenanigans. The menu is a straight-up steaks, seafood, burgers, and chicken affair that is consistently very good.

Yesterdays Café, 435 Oregon Shortline Rd., Dell; (406) 276-3308; $. Yesterdays Café, or the Calf-A, as most folks know it, is located in a one-room brick schoolhouse complete with bell tower and bell. It's a home-cooked sort of menu that features an assortment of daily pies and soups. The rolls and burger buns are baked on the spot and if you're lucky, you might get a homemade doughnut. The cafe is located in a true middle-of-nowhere spot, so baking bread on site is the only option, as commercial deliveries don't come often. Still, if you are on Interstate 15 between Idaho and Montana, it's worth taking the off-ramp for a hearty meal. The building itself is like a rural museum; the unmistakable shape of the schoolhouse structure is telltale of the 1903 one-room prairie school it once was. Built from locally made brick in 1903, it served students from kindergarten through eighth grade until 1963. The building, inside and out, remains much the same as it was eighty years ago. The cook writes daily lunch specials and a list of freshly baked pies on the old chalkboards; the hardwood floors show the scuffs of over a century of bootsteps, and on the shelves schoolbooks stand as a reminder of the past.

Brewpubs & Microbreweries

Blackfoot River Brewing Company, 66 South Park Ave., Helena; (406) 449-3005; www.blackfootriverbrewing.com. With the slogan "Real good beer, made by real good people," it's near impossible not to seek out one of these microbrews, for posterity's sake, at the very least. But with the first gulp you'll get your money's worth in this friendly, well-loved taproom. Daily tap specials and free three-ounce samples keep the house full; Blackfoot also sells beer to go by the growler and will arrange brewery tours by appointment.

Brewmaster and part owner Brian Smith proudly touts Blackfoot as Montana's only certified organic brewery for two of his beers—North Fork Organic Porter and Blackfoot River Gold Organic Pale Ale. The other eight brews are very tasty, of course; typically four of the handcrafted beers are on tap at the pub. Missouri River Steamboat Lager has been the brewery's flagship beer since it opened in 1998. Look for the tap handles at local bars and restaurants.

Brewhouse Pub & Grille, 939½ Getchell St., Helena; (406) 457-9390; www.helenabrewhouse.com. This restaurant occupies the upper floor of the same building as Lewis & Clark Brewing. There's no direct connection between the two businesses, but the brewpub features Lewis & Clark products on the beer list and has twenty microbrews on tap. Through the large windows in the pub, customers can look down and watch Lewis & Clark's head brewer, T. J. Staples, crafting beers. The menu is large and oriented toward beer fare—hearty and running the full range of fish 'n' chips, ribs, pizza, burgers, steaks, and seafood.

Lewis & Clark Brewing, 939 Getchell St., Helena; (406) 442-5960; www.lewisandclarkbrewing.com. When owner Max Pigman markets his brews, he'll talk about the extra hoppy flavor of the Tumbleweed IPA (award-winning time and again) first, but there's a spirit to all his beers that gives the brewery its great reputation. The Miner's Gold Hefeweizen is available in twelve-ounce glass bottles in grocery stores, along with the flagship brands Lewis and Clark Lager, Back Country Scottish Ale, Tumbleweed IPA, and Yellowstone Beer in six-packs. In the taproom, which has a mining shaft motif, two special beers are offered in addition to the regular lineup. Upstairs, the Brewhouse serves great food to accompany L&C ales.

Brewing in Montana Territory

In the Old West, town meetings, dances, festivals, weddings, and even church services were held in the breweries and saloons, which were often the only buildings large enough to hold whole communities. Montana has a long history of breweries: in the late 1800s, few states had more breweries and saloons per capita than Montana. By 1884, breweries were established in Bannack, Billings, Blackfoot, Bozeman, Butte, Deer Lodge, Fort Benton, Glendive, Milestown, Missoula, Philipsburg, Radersburg, Silverbow, Sun River, Townsend, and of course Helena. But the first and oldest was in Virginia City (the 1865 capital of Montana Territory).

Quarry Brewing, 45 West Galena St., Butte; (406) 723-0245. Behind the green door of this very cool-looking industrial building in uptown Butte is what Quarry owners Chuck Schnabel and his wife, Lyza, call a true mom 'n' pop business—they are the only two employees. Just opened in 2007, they enjoy their small craft brewer status, although that may soon change, given the great response to their beers. Butte has a deep history of breweries, long closed, but revived with Chuck's passion for making beer. He brews four basic beers—amber, gold, pale ale, and porter—and two seasonals each year. Galena Gold is a popular light, crisp, easy-drinking summer beer and is available in many local establishments. Quarry regulars seem to prefer Shale Pale Ale. Those regulars get the special treatment: the 150-member Mug Club (there's a waiting list) gets to sample the first batches as they come out.

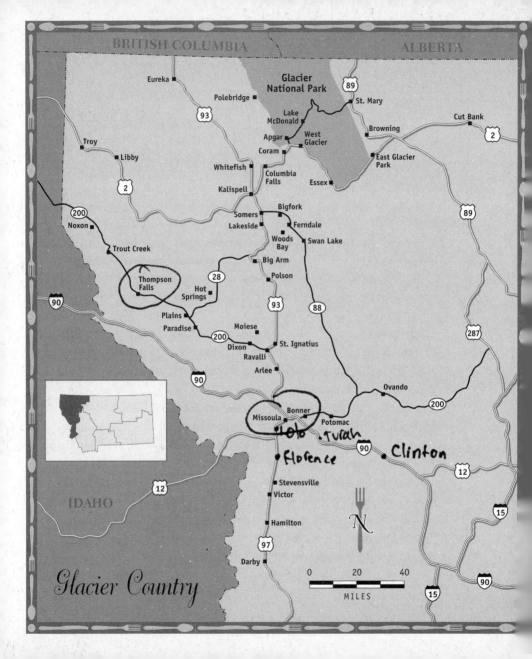

Glacier Country

Glacier Country (Northwest)

This corner of Montana is the most densely populated and likely the most geographically diverse. The southern portion runs along the Idaho border into Missoula, dubbed "the Garden City" for its relatively mild winters. From the Missoula Valley, where the Clark Fork River is joined by the Bitterroot and Blackfoot Rivers, lush farmland fans out toward Arlee and the Rattlesnake Wilderness Area, up along Highway 200 and south to the Bitterroot Valley of Hamilton and Darby. The abundance of produce at farmers' markets served by independent farms from the surrounding region showcases the fertility of the soil here. Melons, cherries, huckleberries, and raspberries overflow from the stands come mid-July, unlike in any other area in the state.

Up from Missoula into Flathead Lake Country, the Mission Mountains and the Swan Range dramatically encircle the largest freshwater lake in the West and create a banana belt for local growers. The mild climate around Flathead changes drastically within 100 miles, as Glacier National Park's remarkable scenery emerges as "the crown of the continent." Entering from the east is almost more striking, as you travel along the Montana Hi-Line from the vast rolling plains through East Glacier and into the steep mountain extremes. Along the way are cafes, seasonal fruit stands, ranches, farms, and historic hotels that serve up their own slice of Montana. From the urban college community of Missoula to the homespun friendliness of small mountain towns, you'll find a plate of something good.

Made or Grown Here

 Big Sky Tea Company, 6107 Montana Highway 200, Thompson Falls; (406) 827-2469. Steven Simonson and his family grow all the herbs for these delicate teas—peppermint, chamomile, echinacea, and spearmint—the herbal classics. Big Sky Tea products are sold in 165 stores across Montana and the Pacific Northwest (or by mail: 6107 Montana Highway 200, Thompson Falls, MT 59873-9418).

Clark Fork Organics, 3507 South 7th St. West, Missoula; (406) 543-1255. For nearly two decades, Clark Fork Organics has sold specialty spring salad greens, herbs, broccoli, chard, cucumber, tomatoes, and squash at the Missoula farmers' market. Farmers Kim Murchison and Josh Slotnick cultivate their six acres using organic practices, with the help of chickens for pest control and goats for weed suppression. The produce is also available at the Good Food Store, the Missoula Community Cooperative, at local restaurants, and through the Western Montana Grower's Cooperative.

Country Pasta, Inc., 46835 U.S. Highway 93, Polson; (406) 883-4384; www.countrypasta.com. Put away the rolling pins and drying racks, the pasta maker, the hours of labor you'd devote to making your own noodles. Country Pasta steps in to bring you that homemade freshness. They make old-fashioned pasta with only the highest-quality ingredients: semolina ground from durum wheat, fresh eggs, natural sea salt, and clean mountain water. Started by husband and wife team Dean and Linda Knutson in 1990, Country Pasta offers two products, Homemade Style Country Pasta and Wide Egg Pasta, both hand-rolled and hand-cut. The business has been sold to a new owner recently, but they prefer to herald the legacy of the Knutson's, who began the business as farmers growing their own wheat. The freshest pasta (next to making it yourself) is available every Friday through Country Pasta, as long as you place your order on Wednesday and can pick it up in person. Otherwise, look for Country Pasta at groceries across the country or directly from the Web site.

Country Pasta Alfredo

16 ounces Country Pasta egg noodles, uncooked
1 cup (2 sticks) butter
1½ cups heavy cream
Salt and pepper to taste
1 dash garlic salt
1¼ cups assorted grated Italian cheeses (Parmesan, Romano)

1. Cook the pasta according to the package directions and drain.
2. In a large saucepan, combine butter and cream; melt over low heat, stirring constantly.
3. Add the salt, pepper, and garlic salt. Stir in the cheese over medium heat until melted.
4. Toss the pasta with the Alfredo sauce to thoroughly coat. Serve immediately.

Serves 6.

Country Pasta, Inc.
46835 U.S. Highway 93, Polson
(406) 883-4384
www.countrypasta.com

Dixon Melons, Inc., 11067 Montana Highway 200, Dixon; (406) 246-3526; www.dixonmelons.com. On nineteen acres in western Montana, Harley Hettick and his family typically plant 40,000 melon starts each April. A good year will yield around 200,000 melons so sweet and delicate you won't want to eat another melon unless you grow it yourself. The key is the picking: the Hetticks know just when to pick these luscious fruits. Varieties such as Crenshaws, muskmelon, honeydew, red and yellow watermelon, and some unusual hybrids are allowed to ripen on the vine to edible perfection.

Farmer Hettick tells great stories about his twenty years as a melon farmer selling at local markets. During August and September people start looking for the Dixon Melon trucks, hoping for a taste of the mouthwateringly sweet muskmelons (cantaloupe) and yellow watermelon or Harley's secret hybrid, The Sinful. The melons grown at this family operation are sold in major grocery stores and small markets in Hamilton, Stevensville, Missoula, Polson, Charlo, Kalispell, Whitefish, and even Bozeman. For the full effect, travel to Dixon for the Melon Day Festival in August, when the whole town celebrates their prize harvest.

Garden City Fungi, P.O. Box 159, Missoula; (406) 626-5757; www.gardencityfungi.com. It's hard to describe the pleasure of successfully growing your own mushrooms at home (especially if you are as green-thumb challenged as this food writer) and then harvesting them to cook for a meal. I'll just say that the boxes of dirt and spores that come from Garden City are definitely sealed with a satisfaction guarantee. The company offers a full line of mushroom growing kits for shiitakes, oysters, and lion's manes, among others. Founded by Missoula farmers in 1995, Garden City specializes in the cultivation of certified-organic gourmet 'shrooms on a completely indoor farm that produces fresh mushrooms year-round

Gluten Free Mama's
Honey Sandwich Bread

1 cup warm water (105–115°F)
1 tablespoon sugar
1 tablespoon yeast
3 cups Gluten Free Mama's
    Rice Almond Blend Flour
2 teaspoons xanthan gum

¾ teaspoon salt
2 tablespoons butter
⅓ cup honey
⅓ cup applesauce, at room
    temperature
1 teaspoon cider vinegar

1. Spray a 4 x 8-inch bread pan with nonstick spray. In a liquid measuring cup, combine warm water, sugar, and yeast. Stir and set aside until foamy, about 5 minutes.
2. In a stand mixer bowl, combine flour, xanthan gum, and salt. Stir to combine.
3. Melt butter in the microwave, 15–20 seconds. Measure out honey, applesauce, and vinegar. With mixer running on low speed, slowly

under controlled conditions. Garden City also harvests wild morel and chanterelle mushrooms when in season. Mushroom kits can be mail-ordered or found in regional natural food stores.

Gluten Free Mama Kitchen, 509 3rd St., Polson; (406) 883-6426; www.glutenfreemama.com. From mixes for pizza crust to pancake batter to flour mixes made of coconut or almond, this pour yeast mixture into dry ingredients. With mixer continuing on low speed, pour in butter, honey, applesauce, and vinegar. Stop mixer and scrape down sides of bowl. Beat on high speed for 3 minutes.

4. Spread dough evenly into prepared bread pan. Smooth out top. Cover with towel and place in warm area to rise for 1–1½ hours, or until doubled in size.

5. Preheat the oven to 375°F. Place pan on second lowest rack in oven. Bake for 30 minutes, then without removing from oven, cover with foil and continue baking 30 minutes longer. (Foil prevents overbrowning.) Wait at least 30 minutes before slicing bread for best results.

Gluten Free Mama tip: Store honey at room temperature out of direct sunlight. If honey crystallizes, return it to its liquid state by placing it in a pan of hot water briefly.

Makes 1 loaf.

Gluten Free Mama Kitchen
509 3rd St., Polson
(406) 883-6426
www.glutenfreemama.com

pioneering cottage industry is dedicated to making a gluten-free diet tastier. Owner Rachel Carlyle-Gauthier developed her recipes and specialty products in response to her daughter's diagnosis with gluten intolerance and thought that other people might appreciate the same good food substitutes.

Folks with gluten allergies or celiac disease don't have to miss out on all the treats any longer. Gluten Free Mama has developed some delicious combinations that will satiate any food lover—with or without allergies. The products are available on her Web site and also in natural food markets from Oregon to Texas. *Gluten Free Mama's Best Baking Recipes Cookbook* along with Mama's Almond Blend Flour and Mama's Coconut Blend Flour make eating enjoyable again.

Howling Moon Salsa & Specialty Foods, P.O. Box 8615, Missoula; (406) 493-0681; www.howlingmoonsalsa.com. The weekly "Taco Night" in Starla Gade's family kitchen was anticipated for the home cooking and company as much as for the salsa.

FOOD LOVERS' TIP

In a good year, the huckleberries are abundant on mountain trails above 5,000 feet. Hikers share secret patches with grizzly bears and other territorial beasts trying to gobble up the berries before they dry on the bush. Similar to blueberries, but smaller and tangier, huckleberries grow in the wild and are a regional delicacy. In the best summers, harvesters pay crews of pickers to scour the mountainsides for the "crop" and sell them at roadside stands that dot the northern portion of the state (along Highway 38 and around the loop on Flathead Lake). The local pickers call huckleberries "purple gold" because a pound usually sells for between $15 and $30, but in poor harvest years they can fetch almost $50.

Friends encouraged Gade to sell her fresh salsas at the farmers' market, where she tested her tried-and-true recipes in 2002. Since then, her product line has grown, and it now includes all-natural salsas in Medium, Hot, Blazin', Smokin' Chipotle, Salsa Verde, and Trail Lovers Black Bean and Corn. She also added fruit salsas: Mango Tango, Sweet & Spicy Pineapple, and Montana Huckleberry Chipotle. Then a list of cooking sauces: Enchilada Sauce, Blazin' Glazin, and Hot Sauce. And dry seasonings, too: Taco Seasoning, Big Sky Bean Dip, Salsa Cruda, Howling Chili, Chipotle Ranch Dip, and Fajita Seasoning. Now she sells at the Saturday Clark Fork River Market in Missoula and the Bitterroot Valley Farmer's Market in Hamilton. Folks flock to her booth for samples of her flavorful salsas during the summer months. The rest of the year, Gade and her family sell via Internet orders and at retail outlets nearby, such as the Good Food Store in Missoula, Bitterroot Emporium in Hamilton, and Bitterroot Community Market in Stevensville.

Huckleberry Haven, P.O. Box 5160, Kalispell; (406) 756-5525. Specializing in all things huckleberry since 1987, Huckleberry Haven handpicks every flavor-bursting berry from the wilderness near Glacier Park. The Huckleberry Jam is work to seek out, but add to that the chocolate-dipped berries, tea, and flavored coffee, and you have a pure Montana moment. The products are available at several national parks, including Glacier National Park, Yellowstone National Park, Grand Teton National Park, Yosemite National Park, and Mount Rushmore National Park, as well as online.

Lifeline Farm and Dairy, 2424 Meridian Rd., Victor; (406) 642-9717; www.lifelinefarm.com. Before there was a trend toward buying organic, healthy, and local foods, Lifeline Farm began in 1978 in Victor, with the intention of growing nutritious, organic, and biodynamic foods to nourish people in the community and throughout the United States.

Today Lifeline Farm, Inc. is a partnership between three of the early members, Ernie Harvey, Luci Breiger, and Steve Elliot. The farm has formed two distinct parts, Lifeline Dairy and Lifeline Produce. Ernie Harvey manages a herd of about 400 Brown Swiss cows, bulls, calves, and steers for Lifeline Dairy. Ernie sells at Missoula and Bitterroot farmers' markets, offering a table filled with his own cheddar, Brie, cheese curds, and other farm cheeses, alongside a freezer full of beef, lamb, and pork products. Many grocery and health food stores around Montana carry Lifeline goods, as well, and they are available online at the Web site.

Mannix Family Beef, 83 Mannix Ranch Dr., Helmville; (406) 793-5585. At Missoula's Clark Fork River Market on Saturdays in the summer, you'll see a good-natured cowboy smiling as he tells about the Mannix Brothers Ranch. Ranch manager Scott Barger knows this fifth-generation ranching family values the land and producing healthy grass-fed beef that's better for everyone. Meat is available at the market, at natural food stores, and directly from the ranch.

Montana Coffee Traders, 5810 Highway 93 South, Whitefish; (800) 345-5282 or (406) 862-7633; www.coffeetraders.com. A bad cup of coffee turned out to be a great inspiration for R.C. Beall. In 1981, before the specialty coffee trend had become mainstream in the U.S., he started with a small home roaster and Montana Coffee Traders was born.

From a restored old farmhouse, Montana Coffee roasts beans fresh daily and sends out orders each day to cities around the world. But Beall's business has grown beyond Montana; he's established roasting companies in Texas, Costa Rica, and several other locations in the U.S.

Offering certified-organic coffees and teas, Montana Coffee Traders produces small batches of fresh roasted coffee in more than 175 varieties of roasts, blends, flavors, and decafs—from around the world. What started in a small farmhouse has grown into a bigger industry. Look for the products in Town & Country grocery stores throughout the state (or online) and in coffee shops in Whitefish, Kalispell and Colombia Falls.

Montana Gourmet Garlic, 2711 Snyder Rd., Stevensville; (406) 777-1566; www.montanagourmetgarlic.com. Garlic is not just for keeping the vampires away; any food lover knows that. For Mary Jane Ross and Christin Rzasa, garlic is a passion that they transformed into a unique niche business. From the Bitterroot Valley, they grow gourmet garlic, known as "hardneck" garlic for its robust flavor. They follow organic gardening practices and sell their wares at local farmers' markets, as well as from their Web site.

Montana SweetHeat, 115½ South 4th St. West, Missoula; (406) 542-0622; www.montanasweetheat.com. From the owners of Montana's first Indian food restaurant (Tipu's Tiger) come these products, which appear in the dishes at the restaurant. After numerous requests for recipes, owner Bipin Patel decided to put them in bottles. Look for SweetHeat flavors around Missoula: roasted habañero honey in four flavors (original, lemon, piña colada, and huckleberry) and roasted habañero-huckleberry BBQ glaze.

Montana Tom's Gift Emporium, 137 Central Ave., Whitefish; (406) 863-9108; www.montanatom.com. Producing everything from fudge to trout with chocolate rocks to Pie in a Jar, Tom Krustangel has been creating confections for over a decade, crafting his products as novelty gifts. With three locations (a shop in Whitefish, another at Whitefish Mountain Ski Resort, and the factory in Thompson Falls), his fudge, ice cream, and delectable milk chocolates are very accessible.

Montana Treasures, 35071 Repass Trail, St. Ignatius; (877) 204-0779; www.montanatreasures.com. For a wild berry that is hard to find and not possible to cultivate, the huckleberry sure can be used to make many *different* treats. The folks at Montana Treasures see to it that no huckleberry goes to waste. They sell huckleberry gummi bears, chocolate, flavored cocoa, jam, cordials, and huckleberry crunch and cheesecake jelly beans, as well as syrup, coffee beans, and pancake mix flavored with (what else?) huckleberries.

Golden Whitefish Caviar Blini

1½ cups milk
1 teaspoon sugar
1 envelope (¼ ounce) active dry
    yeast
¾ cup buckwheat flour
¾ cup all-purpose flour
½ teaspoon salt

4 tablespoons unsalted butter,
    melted
Melted butter, for griddle
3 large egg yolks
2 large egg whites
Sour cream, for garnish
2 4-ounce jars Golden
    Whitefish Caviar

1. Heat milk in a small saucepan until lukewarm. Transfer to large bowl, stir in sugar and yeast, and let stand until the mixture looks creamy (about 5 minutes).
2. Whisk in flour, salt, butter, and egg yolks until smooth.
3. Cover tightly with plastic wrap and let rise in a warm place until doubled (about 1 hour).
4. In a separate bowl, beat egg whites until stiff and fold into batter.
5. Heat 1 tablespoon butter in a nonstick pan or skillet over medium-low heat until melted. Spoon 1 tablespoon of batter at a time, 1 inch apart onto pan. Cook for about 1 minute or until edges are golden brown. Turn and cook for 30 seconds. Keep in warm oven covered loosely with foil until ready to serve.
6. Serve blinis topped with a dollop of sour cream and a spoonful of Golden Whitefish Caviar.

Makes 4 dozen.

Mountain Lake Fisheries
P.O. Box 1067, Columbia Falls
(888) 809-0826
www.whitefishcaviar.com

Grow Montana

In 2001 a group of growers banded together to find a way to distribute their products to the wholesale market. They wanted to be able to deliver fresh, healthy, local produce and meats to the community. Now, fifteen member farms supply a wide range of products to restaurants, groceries, and some local schools in western Montana, from the Bitterroot to Glacier, from Missoula to Helena. Their products include organic fresh fruits and vegetables, some processed fruits and vegetables, organic dairy products, local honey, and a variety of meats: organic poultry and natural beef, pork, and bison. The Web site is a great resource for consumers who want to learn about local farmers and the benefits of sustaining communities by shopping locally.

Western Montana Growers Cooperative
P.O. Box 292, Arlee
(406) 726-4769
www.wmgcoop.com

Mountain Lake Fisheries, P.O. Box 1067, Columbia Falls; (888) 809-0826; www.whitefishcaviar.com. Anglers groan when they net another mountain whitefish on the lakes and rivers of Montana. The sucker look-alike is considered a nuisance by most fishermen, who quickly toss the fish back or kill it on the spot. They are viewed as invasive and ruinous of trout and Kokanee salmon habitat. But

Mountain Lake Fisheries owner Ronald Mohn turned them into a thriving business, selling Montana Golden Whitefish Caviar, Lake Whitefish Fillets, and "Montana Fixin's" (a dry deep-fry batter mix). Begun in 1991, Mountain Lake Fisheries practices the only rod and reel commercial whitefish harvesting operation in the country—and produces what some say is the best caviar in the world.

Paradise Gardens, P.O. Box 87, Paradise; (406) 826-4242. Combining beauty and flavor, Ted and Paula Seaman grow organic vegetables and edible flowers on their twenty-acre farm in the warmest microclimate in Montana. Pansies, nasturtiums, calendula, begonias, lavender, and other flowers create delicious, healthful salad combinations that are as pretty as a bouquet. They sell to local restaurants, in grocery stores throughout Idaho and Montana, and at farmers' markets from June through September. You can also call ahead to make an appointment to tour the greenhouse and gardens.

Silent Creations Buffalo Products, 43299 Round Butte Rd., Ronan; (406) 381-1498; www.indianbuffalojerky.com. Mesquite-smoked and flavorful, this buffalo jerky is made from Montana buffalo that are hormone- and antibiotic-free. Owner Matthew Silent Thunder is a Mescalero Apache and of German descent, and he notes that buffalo is a symbol of pride and strength for Native American people. In that vein, he produces jerky in a traditional style with no added preservatives. Order online or buy a pack from a Montana convenience store for a high-protein snack.

Uncle Bill's Sausages, 1918 Brooks St., Missoula; (406) 543-5627. Desperate for good sausage in Montana, Bill Stoianoff resorted to making it himself fifteen years ago. Today he shows his passion for charcuterie at the Clark Fork River Market every Saturday during the summer months or from his eclectic hippie shop, The Joint Effort, any time. In addition to sausage, he makes a very fine sweet-spicy dry barbecue rub for ribs or other meaty treats.

Wild Rose Emu Ranch, www.wildroseemu.com. This writer will confess that the novelty of "emu ranching" is just too irresistible not to include in a food lovers' guide. Yet, all smirking aside, emu meat has become highly marketable and the other products derived from the animals make for a highly productive crop. Started in 1996, and home to approximately 120 emus, Wild Rose Emu Ranch has taken agriculture to a new level. The bird is 95 percent usable, providing a healthy red meat as well as a remarkable oil for the skin; a strong, supple leather; silky and bristly feathers; and 5½-inch dark green eggs. From facial creams to shoe leather, this flightless bird is a useful commodity.

Joe and Clover Quinn take pride in the care they give their emus, the attention they provide their customers, and the delight of those who tour the ranch for the first time, as well as the repeat visitors. They sell their products direct from the Web site and nearby Hamilton Bitterroot Grocery & Emporium, Rainbow's End, Bitterroot Drug, Hamilton Pharmacy, Healthcare Plus Pharmacy, and Natural Beginnings all carry emu products. Other locations include Canyon Salon in Missoula and Stevensville's Bitterroot Community Market.

Big Dipper Ice Cream, 631 South Higgins Ave., Missoula; (406) 543-5722; www.bigdippericecream.com. It seems enough to say that this little place makes the best milk shakes. Perfectly thick. Rich. You'll want to savor yours. Then, when you slurp to the end, you'll feel great, guilty satisfaction. Sure, they've got your homemade chocolate and vanilla, but I'm a sucker for Mexican Chocolate (dark and cinnamony). Other specialty flavors made here since 1995 are Cardamom, Espresso Heath, Lime Margarita Sherbet, and White Mint Oreo, among many, many others. Available in eighty-seven-ounce "growlers" is Huckleberry, the best seller, hands down, according to owner Charlie Beaton. But also in the running must be the Flathead Cherry or the local Dixon Honeydew Melon Sorbet.

Big Sky Candy, 319 West Main St., Hamilton; (866) 432-8282 or (406) 363-0580; www.bigskycandy.com. At Big Sky Candy, sweet treats are serious business. Professional confectioners craft handmade choc- olates, truffles, creams, toffees, cinnamon-glazed almonds, and fun concoctions the old-fashioned way—from scratch, at the right temperature, with the exact amount of handling required to create perfection. Since 2001 John and Michele DeGroot have made Big Sky Bars, Elk Eyes, Hay Stacks, Beaver Dams—all chocolate specialties that echo with Montana's influence and are worth a taste test.

Charbonneau's Chocolate Shop, 755 Main St., Stevensville; (406) 777-0808; www.charbonneauschocolate.com. From chocoholics to chocolatiers—this out-of-the-way shop uses family recipes to create one-of-a-kind confections. Founder Sally "Alex" Johnson stepped out of the daily business operations and handed the shop on to her daughter, Sheila Schiwal, in 2005. Carrying on the tradition, Charbonneau's produces over 150 varieties of delicious hand-dipped chocolates, truffles, confections, and Montana novelties. Be sure to ask about summer day camps for cupcake bakers and home candymakers.

Colter Coffee House and Roasting, 424 Main St., Kalispell; (406) 755-1319; www.coltercoffee.com. Voted the best coffee in the Flathead Valley—repeatedly—Colter Coffee has a central location in downtown Kalispell in a classic brick building that's been renovated to have a slightly hip city ambience. Colter roasts beans on site and sells them in a varied assortment of drinks. Request the Cowboy Cappuccino to feel like a local.

Eva Gates Homemade Preserves, 456 Electric Ave., Bigfork; (800) 682-4283 or (406) 837-4356; www.evagates.com. Nothing fancy, just good, these homemade huckleberry syrups and preserves are artfully prepared. And there's good history to the products, too. It all started in 1949 with a bumper crop in Eva Gates's strawberry patch. She made some preserves and gave them to the neighbors; it became a tradition. Pretty soon, folks were asking if they could buy another jar, and after selling a lot of jars, Eva decided to make it a business. Today her granddaughter Gretchen Gates carries on the tradition from a cute country cottage on Bigfork's main street. You can also buy the strawberry preserves (and huckleberry, too) online.

 Good Food Store, 1600 South 3rd St. West, Missoula; (406) 541-3663; www.goodfoodstore.com. This independently owned store gives the Whole Foods chain a run for its money. With a strong local clientele and sustainable food movement, it is a community-centric natural food grocery store with full-service deli, a large bulk department, and a wide selection of natural and organic food. Look for labels on local meats and fish, detailing where the products are produced. There is also a nice organic wine and cheese selection here.

Great Northern Foods, 425 Grand Dr. in the Grand Hotel, Bigfork; (406) 837-2715; www.grandhotelbigfork.com. The coffee is Starbucks, but the exceptional pastries, muffins, and croissants are baked fresh daily in this gourmet deli on the first floor of the Grand Hotel in downtown Bigfork. Owner and chef Neil Navratil creates gourmet meals to go, along with offering the perfect array of wines and specialty groceries for that picnic on the lake. The imported cheese and superb wine selection are essential to said picnic.

Helen's Candies, 1407 Minnesota Ave., Libby; (406) 293-4687. Who can resist a huckleberry cordial? You must pop the whole thing into your mouth (no dainty bites allowed) and let the sweet syrup burst across your taste buds. Helen's also makes chocolate-covered cherries, caramel, peanut brittle, and preserves.

M & S Meats, 23691 U.S. Highway 93, Rollins; (406) 844-3414; www.msmeats.com. Cooler shelves are stacked with a multitude of varieties of meats, cheeses, and sausages. Offering Montana buffalo sausage, elk steaks, and jerky, along with a sixty-year-old recipe for barbecue sauce, this roadside stop is full of surprises. Lucy Carlson, the proprietor, practices her butchering skills with pride in one of the area's long-running businesses. Established in 1945, locals know it as the best place to order a special cut of meat for the holidays or bring wild game for artful processing.

Missoula Community Food Co-op, 1500 Burns St., Missoula; (406) 728-2369; www.missoulafoodcoop.com. "Food to the people" could be the slogan at this community-run grocery. A description of their membership says, "Membership to the budding co-op is a commitment to community, sustainability, and economic justice." That is to say that good, healthy food requires commitment. This cooperatively run grocery has been operated by members since

Tips for Cooking Bison from the Missoula Community Food Co-op

Bison is stunningly tasty, lean, and healthy. It is available in many forms from local humane producers throughout the state. Check out the National Bison Association site (www.bisoncentral.com).

Try a bison steak! No worries, it's not hard to cook. The trick is to not overcook; it's best to go rare or medium rare. If you like your steak more well done (I do), no worries. It will be a little drier than beef cooked well but still really tasty and healthy.

Here's how: Rub your steaks with salt, fresh cracked pepper, and a little onion and garlic powder. Place in a hot heavy metal pan with hot olive oil and sear. Reduce heat to medium high after a couple of minutes, and cook until steaks are at desired doneness. Steaks are also good done on a grill if cooked over hot coals or flames. Marinating the steaks will help keep the meat moist if it's done on the grill, but this is not absolutely required.

2006. Not only does the co-op provide all the wonderful specialty fare we foodies have come to crave (read: artisanal cheese, pre-made sauces, beautiful bulk food bins, quality meat, poultry, and seafood), but it has bolstered the local food system network by showcasing regional products wherever possible. Aside from the delightful retail offerings, the co-op has assembled a remarkable database listing contact information for farms in the Bitterroot, Flathead, Mission, and Missoula areas. Detailing more than thirty farms that range from biodynamic and certified organic to conventional or simply homegrown, the database lists everything from legumes to licorice tea.

Montana Buffalo Gals, 166 Highway 212, Dixon; (406) 246-7777. Montana Buffalo Gals, Inc. was formed in 2001 with the intention of selling wholesome, ranch-raised buffalo meat. The herd of seventy or so animals roams 110 acres, two miles from Dixon. Montana Buffalo Gals meat is available at the Missoula Community Food Co-op.

Old World Delicatessen, 103B 3rd Ave. East, Polson; (406) 883-2245. This classic deli with meats, cheese, marinated salads, some prepared sub sandwiches, and frozen homemade entrees, along with homemade desserts to go, offers most of its food to be carried out. You'll find imported meats and cheeses like prosciutto di Parma, salami, Italian-style coppa both hot and mild, mortadella, Parmesan, Spanish blue, and Gouda. And if you have a special request, proprietor Joan Platko will order it if possible.

Uncorked Wines, 60 Commons Way, Kalispell; (406) 257-WINE (9463). Reds, whites, tons of organic varietals, and sparkling wines fill the racks at Ron Scharfe's gem of a shop. The cheese selection alone (thirty-five different types last time I checked) should bring the locals in at least weekly. Jazz music plays in the background to put you in the mood for any one of the current

offerings, some recommended through the monthly wine club and others by the wine experts here. A fantastic deli stocks cured meats, olives, and pâtés to accompany the wine selection of the day.

This place is badass Like for real.

Worden's Market, 451 North Higgins Ave., Missoula; (406) 549-1293; www.wordens.com. Wine, beer, groceries, deli, and cigars—what *else* is there? Worden's is a downtown institution for foodies in Missoula. And it comes with a side of history: It was established around 1883, as Missoula's first grocery store. While it was known for staples in the old days, today the deli caters and offers delicious sandwiches (think Genoa salami, smoked turkey, and things with artichokes on them). Each department (wine, beer, food, smokes) has a resident expert for any questions or requests.

Farmers' Markets

Bigfork Farmers' Market Cooperative, 400 Commerce (Bigfork High School Parking Lot), Bigfork. One of the best markets in the state. Saturday 10 a.m. to 2 p.m., May through October; Wednesday 4 p.m. to 7 p.m., June through August.

Clark Fork River Market, Downtown Missoula next to the Clark Fork River in Caras Park. Saturday 8 a.m. to 1 p.m., May through October. Cooking or gardening demonstrations are offered weekly from 10 a.m. to 11 a.m.

Darby Farmers Market, on the corner of U.S. Highway 93 and Tanner St. Tuesday 4 p.m. to 6 p.m., May through October.

Eureka Farmer's Market, Riverside Park. Saturday 9 a.m. to 1 p.m., May through September.

Harvest Valley Farmers' Market, 3rd and Main Streets, Stevensville. Saturday 9 a.m. to 1 p.m. and the first Friday of the month 5 p.m. to 9 p.m., end of April through mid-October.

Kalispell Farmers' Market, Center Mall parking lot at Center St. and 5th Ave., Kalispell. One of the earliest openers and the latest closers of all markets in the state. Saturday 9 a.m. to 12:30 p.m., third week in April through third week in October.

Kootenai Country Farmers' Market, band shell on Mineral Ave., Libby. Thursday 4 to 7 p.m., June through September.

Littlebirds Marketplace, Larch Ln. on the lawn at Littlebirds, Seeley Lake. Sunday 10 a.m. to 2 p.m., June through September.

Missoula Farmer's Market, Circle Square on North Higgins Ave., downtown Missoula. Saturday 9 a.m. to noon, mid-May through mid-October. Tuesday 5:45 to 7:15 p.m., July through August.

Plains Paradise Farmers' Market, Sanders County Fairground, Plains. Saturday 9 a.m. to noon, June through September.

Polson Farmer's Market, Masonic Temple parking lot, 1102 4th Ave. East, Polson. Friday 9 a.m. to 1 p.m., May through October.

Ronan Farmers' Market, Chamber Visitor Center, Highway 93, Ronan. Friday 4 to 7 p.m., May through late September.

Thompson Falls Market, west lot of the Falls Motel, Lincoln St. and Maiden Ln., ½ block west of Highway 200/Main St., Thompson Falls. Saturday 9 a.m. to 1 p.m., July through the second weekend of October.

Valley Farmers Market, Bedford St. (2 blocks south of Main, between 2nd and 3rd St.), Hamilton. Saturday 9 a.m. to 12:30 p.m., May through October.

West End Farm & Craft Market, Bicentennial Park, 179 Railroad Rd., Noxon. Saturday 10 a.m. to 2 p.m., June through October.

Whitefish Downtown Farmers Market, Park at the end of Central Ave., Whitefish. Tuesday 5 to 7:30 p.m., May through September.

Whitefish Farmers Market, Pin and Cue parking lot, 6570 Highway 93 South, Whitefish. Thursday 4 to 6:30 p.m., May through September.

Benson's Farm, 2418 South 7th St. (corner of 7th and Reserve St.), Missoula; (406) 543-5061. Missoulians wait all summer long for Benson's white and yellow corn. They pull into the parking lot daily starting the first of August and won't stop until they can buy the fresh-picked ears. This family farm on the edge of bustling Missoula city limits has been producing produce for the public since 1900. Besides the sweet corn, the farm also sells assorted vegetables, pumpkins, and autumn decorations such as gourds, hay bales, cornstalks, and flowers. Usually open 8 a.m. to 6 p.m. from May through November.

Bowman Orchards, 21480 East Shore Route, Bigfork; (406) 982-3246; www.bowmancherries.com. Bowman Orchards is family owned and operated since 1921. A small orchard was started by Adam Bowman and then expanded (and currently operated) by son Gerald and his wife, Marilyn. Third-generation family members are involved in retail marketing and Web site maintenance. They grow wonderfully sweet cherries (Bing, Lambert, Rainier, and Lapin). The retail store also sells cherry jam, syrup, and juice; fudge; dried cherries; and cherry firewood, which is good for smoking meats. The orchard is located just 10 miles south of Bigfork; it's a good idea to call before stopping by.

Branch Ranch, 21263 Montana Highway 35, Yellow Bay; (406) 982-3770. Rick and Diana Nash prioritize growing luscious Flathead Lake cherries without pesticide sprays and are independent sellers. Stop by the cherry stand or find them at farmers' markets. Open from mid-July through August; call for news of ripe fruit.

Fat Robin Orchard and Farm, 34126 South Finley Point Rd., Polson; (406) 887-2869. Lise Rousseau's certified-organic orchard sells cherries from July through August (Lambert, Rainier, Van, Montmorency, and Balaton) and then apples from late September through October (McIntosh, Wealthy, and Wolf River). Fruit is available through the farm, local CSAs, and Montana natural food markets, and it is featured in local fine restaurants. Alternatively, you can pick your own and enjoy some of the best views of Flathead Lake in the valley. Some of this farm's fruit also goes to Ten Spoon Winery for their outstanding Flathead Cherry Dry wine. Open Monday through Sunday 8 a.m. to 7 p.m. from July through October. Call for directions.

Oakenshield Orchard, 2308 Blaine Rd., Potomac; (406) 244-5446. Christine Oakenshield's place is a small orchard of 200 trees. She takes care not to pick the apples until a good frost touches down and brings the sugar level up, allowing the fruit to mature. Only organic sprays are used in the orchard. Christine also sells hand-pressed cider. The hours of operation are limited, but a visit is worth the short drive out of Missoula, to near Bonner. Open September through November; weekdays from 6 p.m. to 8 p.m. and weekends from 9 a.m. to 8 p.m. Call for directions.

O'Farrell Orchards, 19627 East Lake Shore, Bigfork; (406) 982-3429. Less than 20 miles north of Polson, this orchard has one of the latest harvests for the brief season on Flathead Lake—those on the south end ripen last—and one of the most abundant. From cherries to peaches, pears, plums, and nectarines, then finally apples all the way into October, this is a jewel box for you-pickers. Open 8 a.m. to 6 p.m. July through October.

The Orchard at Flathead Lake, 23126 Yellow Bay Ln., Bigfork; (406) 982-3058. Ray and Carol Johnson began growing cherries for Montana cherry fans in 1976 at their orchard near Bigfork. Today, Ray and Carol's children, Bob, Bill, Roy, Terry, Shana, and Gary, have taken the business to a new level. The biggest change is that the orchard is organic and that they sell most of their product at markets and at their own fruit stand. Since they don't ship much of the crop, the fruit is sold fresh from the tree, within a day or so of picking. That means the cherries reach the customer at the prime of their taste—and that is a very *sweet* thing. Look for The Orchard's cherry jams and specialty sauces at local food stores, as well as at their farm stand.

Sweet Pickins Pumpkin Patch, 512 Columbia Falls Stage Rd., Kalispell; (406) 752-2359; www.sweetpickinspumpkinpatch.com.

CRAVING MONTANA'S FLATHEAD LAKE CHERRIES FROM AFAR?

Buy directly from your favorite cherry orchard . . . they'll ship anywhere. During Montana's cherry season, mid-July through early August, you can visit Flathead Lake Cherry Growers' Web site (www.montanacherries.com) and select "Retail Sellers." You'll see contact information for Flathead Lake cherry growers willing to sell and ship Montana cherries and other cherry-related items directly to your home. If you want your grocery chain to offer Flathead Lake cherries, ask them to contact the marketing/sales company DOMEX (509-966-1814) or Flathead Lake Cherry Growers (406-982-3069).

Cherries were first introduced to the Flathead Lake region in 1866—the Lambert variety, known for its deep red color and sweetness. By the 1930s, cherries were being exported from Flathead to stores all over the country. It was determined that cherries flourished in the Flathead Lake region because of the ideal climate. Montana's rocky, well-drained soil and pristine, glacier-fed water supply is well suited for cherry tree growth. Long warm days with plenty of sunshine help develop outstanding fruit. Cool 40–50°F evenings extend the growing season, which allows the fruit to mature over a longer period of time. These conditions contribute to the outstanding taste of Montana cherries. Today, more than a hundred orchards are members of the Flathead Lake Cherry Growers association, producing as much as 7 million pounds of fruit some years and yielding a multimillion dollar industry. Drive along Montana Highway 35, the east side of Flathead Lake, between Polson and Bigfork to find mom 'n' pop stands set up along the roadside—as sure a sign of summer as the June solstice.

Wagon rides, farm animals, hay mazes, and glorious orange-blazed pumpkins in a broad, open field. There's always magic in a you-pick experience and this family-run patch is one of the loveliest in Flathead Valley. The classic red barn is just another detail in the memorable experience that so many school groups and families encounter on this sweet farm. Open from 9 a.m. to 6 p.m. Monday through Saturday (September 22 to October 31) and 1 p.m. to 6 p.m. Sunday. Call for directions.

Wise Owl Orchards, McIntosh Rd., Florence (near Darby); (406) 273-6699. With 450 trees growing in prime apple country, the list of fruits at Wise Owl reads like a box of chocolates: Empire, Goodland, Early Fuji, Jonagold, Arlet, Old McIntosh, Goodmacs, Honeycrisp. Wise Owl also grows black cherries that are ready to pick in mid-July and August. Open spring through autumn. Call for directions.

Food Happenings

APRIL

Pie Auction and Social, Bigfork. Swan River Community Hall, Highway 83. (406) 837-5888; www.bigfork.org. Where else can a pie buy you entry into a party? At this auction and social, prize pies are awarded to the highest bidder to benefit Swan River Community Hall's maintenance and renovation projects. Don't fret if you don't win the pie of your eye; they also sell pie by the slice ($2) and à la mode ($2.50). Admission is one pie or $5 per family.

Taste of Bigfork, Bigfork, downtown. (406) 837-5888; www .bigfork.org. You won't need to bring your own forks to Taste of Bigfork, not even big ones. But do come with a big appetite. This spring event showcases the culinary charisma of a dozen restaurants and twenty chefs from the area. It's a roving feast, allowing you to sample small plates of everything from yam chips to spaetzles to mini pulled pork sandwiches to ravioli to buffalo to homemade gourmet ice cream at different restaurants along Electric Avenue.

MAY

Garden City Brewfest, Missoula. Caras Park. (406) 543-4238; www.missouladowntown.com. Celebrate spring with a cold pint of one of Montana's finest microbrews. But this festival isn't limited to locals; in fact brewmeisters from one end of the country—Hawaii—to the other—Boston—bring their best to Missoula each year. Held downtown in Caras Park, along the banks of the Clark Fork River, this is a family event with a historic carousel and a favorite gathering for all ages. One price buys a keepsake tasting glass that allows you to sample more than sixty different beers. Enjoy food from local vendors, groove to live music, and vote for your favorite brew.

Taste of Belton, West Glacier. (406) 888-5000; www.beltonchalet .com. This is a great way to sample dishes from the seasonal menu, paired with select wines from the wine list. Set in the private dining room of Belton Chalet, this elegant affair offers limited seating and reservations are essential.

JUNE

Out to Lunch, Missoula. Caras Park. (406) 543-4238; www.missouladowntown.com. It's like a picnic with the whole town each week. The annual Out to Lunch Summer Concert Series kicks off in early June each year and continues weekly through August in beautiful Caras Park in downtown Missoula. Fantastic food from local restaurants, bakeries, dessert shops, and farms comes together each Wednesday with live music and great company from 11 a.m. to 2 p.m.

THIS is where it's at. Fun as hell!

JULY

Bitterroot Microbrew Fest, Hamilton. Legion Park. (406) 363-2400; www.bitterrootvalleychamber.com. What's better than a cold brew in the heat of July? Try the microbrew samplers from local Bitterroot Brewpub and nearby Missoula breweries. The Microbrew Fest is a fun, laid-back event that brings the community together for cold beers and live music.

Flathead Cherry Festival, Polson. (406) 883-5969; www.montana cherries.com. From pie-eating contests to a judging of the most unusual food made with cherries—my money is on the Cherry Coke Salad or the Spiced Cherries—this is a local celebration of the prized harvest of the orchards that circle Flathead Lake. There are plenty of cobblers, dumplings, and clafouti recipes, too. Mid-July through mid-August are the bookends of this fruitful season, which is worthy of a two-day festival, complete with parade down Main Street and community-wide revelry in summer's bounty.

Strawberry Festival, Darby. Darby City Park. (406) 381-5114; www .bitterrootvalleychamber.com. Enjoy angel food cake and fresh strawberries and cream at this homey fund-raiser for the Darby Volunteer Fire Department. It's an annual ice cream social that brings the town out to celebrate summer and listen to local musicians.

Yes. It's a thing. Haven't gone. But hey. There ya go

Testicle Festival, Clinton. Rock Creek Lodge. (406) 825-4868; www.testyfesty.com. The largest food festival of its kind, Testy Festy attracts a raucous bunch of revelers for the regional delicacy of "Rocky Mountain oysters," aka fried bull balls, served up with cowboy beans. Battered and deep-fried, they taste like chicken, everyone says. But I think they taste like fried sweetbreads (organs), only tougher. While the music plays day and night, over two and a half tons of this gourmet food are served. Starting small in 1983, the five-day party has grown to attract thousands of fun-loving travelers who participate in a timed all-you-can-eat contest and wild drinking with the most bizarre mix of partiers you may ever encounter, many of them naked and most of them inebriated.

AUGUST

Annual Huckleberry Festival, Trout Creek. (406) 827-3301; www.huckleberryfestival.com. After celebrating the wild berry for three decades, this small town in northwest Montana was proclaimed by the state legislature to be the "Huckleberry Capital of Montana." Vendors sell them by the bucket at this festival, held when the berries are abundant. Referred to as "purple gold" in these parts, since they sometimes sell for as much as $50 per pound, the dark, tangy berry shows up in huckleberry ice cream, on huckleberry pizza, on cheesecake, in drinks, and even as a garnish on Polish dogs.

Annual Raspberry Jam, Arlee. Heart View Center, 31940 Jocko Rd. (406) 726-2030. This family event at Common Ground Farm just north of Missoula offers an early evening event with all-you-can-pick organic raspberries to the sounds of bluegrass. $10 per person, children under twelve free (as long as you pick, then eat).

Annual Wine Festival, Polson. Polson Airport. (800) 845-4251; www.polsonchamber.com. Eat, drink, and do something good for the community. Local restaurants and caterers band together and pair their food with thirty excellent wines from around the world. Ticket sales and proceeds from auction items benefit local nonprofit groups who are invested in helping young girls and women succeed. Launched by the Soroptimist International group of Polson, the tradition started in the 1980s to raise money for educational scholarships for women in the Mission Valley.

Dixon Melon Day Festival, Dixon. (406) 246-0045; www.dixon melons.com. This all-day celebration kicks off with a jovial parade with floats from local garden clubs, the famous Hettick Farms (the growers of Dixon Melons), and many other community members. After that, the day leads to 5K and 10K races, barbecue, live music, melon-eating contests, and horseshoe tournaments and Farmers Olympics, among other playful activities. It's a good wholesome day and the melons are sweeter than you could imagine—in Montana, with the categorically short growing season and long winters, a sweet, vine-ripened melon is surely a thing to celebrate. Farmers Harley and Joey Hettick set up two pickup trucks containing an assortment of melons—yellow and red watermelon, cantaloupe, muskmelon, or honeydew from Dixon Melons—to give away to the 800 to 1,000 revelers who come for the party. The event is free to the public and takes place on Main Street in tiny Dixon, located on Highway 200, near the National Bison Range and 43 miles northwest of Missoula.

Huckleberry Festival, Swan Lake. Swan Lake Campground Area, Highway 83, between mile markers 72 and 73. (406) 886-2003; www .flatheadevents.net. One part ice cream social and one part competitive cooking contest, this annual event brings out some of the best home cooks this side of the Divide. It's all in the name of the elusive wild berry, and while the cooks slave in the kitchen, the rest of us reap the tasty benefits. Bring your own huckleberry concoction or sample the pies baked by the Swan Lake Volunteer Fire Department. Enjoy the pancake breakfast and sizzling barbecue lunch.

Whitefish SNOW Brewfest, Whitefish. Whitefish Mountain Village. (406) 862-2900; www.skiwhitefish.com. With nearly half of the state's microbreweries located between Whitefish and Missoula, it makes sense to have a brewfest for the locals. This one features beers from Great Northern Brewing down the street, but fairly also offers other Montana microbrews on tap. The event is an annual fund-raiser to support the SNOW bus that runs from Whitefish to Whitefish Mountain Ski Resort during the winter months.

SEPTEMBER

Germanfest, Missoula. Pavilion at Caras Park. (406) 532-3240; www.missoulacultural.org. Break out the lederhosen and get ready to polka after sampling nibbles of sauerkraut. Held each year in the historic downtown, this fall festival is christened by the tapping of a keg by Jurgen Knoeller, owner of Missoula's Bayern Brewery. The bratwurst and potato salad are abundant, as is the spirit of fun. This annual ethnic heritage celebration connects Missoula with its sister city, Neckargemund, one of the oldest communities in Germany.

Libby Nordicfest, Libby. Libby Chamber of Commerce: (406) 293-4167; www.libbynordicfest.org. From lutefisk to Swedish meatballs, this annual celebration of Scandinavian heritage is served up with a healthy dose of *lefsa* and love. Head to the spirited burg of Libby, nestled in the Cabinet Mountains next to the rushing Kootenai River, for parades, music, and Fjord horse shows in the spirit of Norway, Finland, Sweden, Denmark, and Iceland. *Uffda!*

Northwest Honey Fest, Stevensville. Lewis and Clark Park. (406) 777-3773; www.northwesthoneyfest.com. A celebration of the honeybee in Montana, this community event features a honey-inspired food tasting; mead (honey wine) and handcrafted honey beer; and a straight-up honey tasting; along with arts, crafts, and music.

Bees in the Herb Garden Dip or Dressing

Use this as a dip for chips, shrimp, ham cubes, vegetables, ripe olives, or pineapple chunks, or use it as a dressing for green or fruit salad. Recipe courtesy of Northwest Honey Fest organizers.

1 pint sour cream
6 tablespoons honey
2 tablespoons orange juice concentrate, thawed and undiluted
2 tablespoons Dijon mustard
2 teaspoons cream-style horseradish

2 teaspoons fresh rosemary, crushed
1 teaspoon fresh chervil, crushed
1 teaspoon fresh basil, crushed
¾ teaspoon salt
½ teaspoon white pepper
¼ teaspoon garlic powder

Combine all ingredients; mix well. Refrigerate, covered, for several hours to blend flavors. Stir before using.

Makes 20 2-tablespoon servings.

Old West Autumnfest, Frenchtown. Opportunity Ranch, 14275 Hamel Rd. (406) 329-1709. In early September remarkable Opportunity Ranch opens to the community. The Autumnfest attracts 3,000 people for wholesome family fun: hayrides, pumpkin picking, dancing, music, farm animals, firefighter displays, exhibits, apple-cider making, and lots of games. Everyone over thirteen pays $5 for the day, with activities going on from 10 a.m. to 4 p.m. All proceeds benefit the ranch operations.

Opportunity Ranch, a 160-acre working ranch for individuals with disabilities, has raised sheep, cattle, pigs, and garden produce since 2004. In recent years the Ranch Crew has raised 3,000 pumpkins for festival activities and sold a variety of wool products, including close to 950 wool blankets, made from a blend of Opportunity Ranch wool. Opportunity Resources, Inc. is a nonprofit community organization serving 400 individuals with disabilities daily, helping with employment, training, housing supports, transportation, and recreation.

NAME THAT LAKE!

According to local history, Lake Kooncanusa (actually a reservoir created by the Libby Dam on the Kootenai River in 1972) was christened through a publicity contest sponsored by the U.S.-Canadian governments, who shared the cost of building the dam. The winner: Alice Beers, from Rexford, Montana, combined the first three letters from KOOtenai River, and the first three letters of CANada and USA.

Salmon Festival, Eureka. 2 Dewey Ave., Historical Village. (406) 889-4636; www.welcome2eureka.com. The salmon festival revolves around the annual Kokanee salmon run up the Tobacco River, which flows through the Historical Village in downtown Eureka from nearby Lake Koocanusa. The salmon cook-off is the highlight of the all-day event, but the fishing derby and casting contest, among other activities, provide plenty of entertainment as well.

Taste of Whitefish, Whitefish. O'Shaughnessy Center, One Central Ave. (406) 862-3501; www.whitefishchamber.com. From sushi to steaks, the restaurants of Whitefish unfurl the tablecloth with some fabulous food. Twenty Whitefish restaurants provide samples, and there's also beer from the Great Northern Brewing Company, a wine tasting with regional vintages, and the great atmosphere of Indian summer in September.

OCTOBER

McIntosh Apple Day, Hamilton. Ravalli County Museum, 205 Bedford St. (406) 363-2400; www.bitterrootvalleychamber.com. Billed as the biggest bake sale under the Big Sky, this is a sweet community harvest festival. A giant farmers' market with arts and crafts and live music showcases fall vegetables, fruits, and lots of specialty food items. Apple butter bubbles over an open fire, fresh-squeezed apple juice is abundant, and the wholesome scent of baked apples of all kinds (pies, crisps, turnovers) permeates the autumn festivities.

A Link in the Chain

Although this book is intended to provide a map to the best local hot spots and out-of-the-way eateries rather than chain restaurants, a few regional franchises that started off as single small-town restaurants are worth noting.

Ciao Mambo! This small but growing chain dishes out peasant Italian dishes with a hearty dose of flash from the exhibition kitchen and the snappy atmosphere. Pizza, pasta, and more specifically, the Nachos Italiana, are satisfying and well priced. The first restaurant opened in Whitefish in 2000; a second location opened in Missoula three years later, securing the concept as a Montana favorite. Whitefish: 234 East Second St.; (406) 863-9600. Missoula: 541 South Higgins Ave.; (406) 543-0377.

MacKenzie River Pizza Company. Since opening its first restaurant in downtown Bozeman in 1993, with a fly-fishing and river-themed concept (a classic MacKenzie River boat hangs from the ceiling in the center of the restaurant), the idea has spread throughout

Montana Master Chefs, Greenough. 40060 Paws Up Rd. (800) 473-0601; www.montanamasterchefs.com. "Glamping." Known for luxurious accommodations, lavish gourmet meals, and a wilderness setting, The Resort at Paws Up epitomizes the contemporary term combining "glamour" and "camping." Frankly, what's not to like? This exclusive, posh resort hosts Montana Master Chefs, an annual foodie retreat that includes four days and three nights in a private the state. MacKenzie River Pizza Company now operates twelve restaurants across Montana and opened a thirteenth store in Coeur d'Alene, Idaho, in 2008. The largest locally owned restaurant group in the state, MacKenzie River is famed for its The Rancher pizza (with a choice of sourdough, natural grain, or thin hand-tossed crust), topped with a heart-stopping amount of ground beef, pepperoni, bacon, red onion, bell pepper, fresh tomatoes, signature tomato sauce, and heaps of mozzarella. www.mackenzieriverpizza.com.

Montana's Rib & Chop House. This growing restaurant group started in little downtown Livingston (305 East Park St.; (406) 222-9200), with a hungry clientele that craved the slow-cooked barbecue ribs and Pasta Jambalaya. The original location still thrives, but new restaurants in Billings and Miles City (and two in Wyoming) have made it easier to find some of the state's best Southern-style barbecue. With a casual atmosphere, generous Montana-size portions, and a menu that appeals to both the finicky and the frivolous, this is the kind of place that is packed from the moment the doors open. www.ribandchophouse.com.

luxury home with breakfast, lunch, and dinner prepared by a different world-class guest chef each day, culminating in the evenings (after hiking, rafting, mountain biking, horseback riding, sporting clays, or ATV adventures) with an exquisite five-course dinner and a wine pairing from a guest winemaker. It's spendy, but absolutely worth the splurge.

Ocktober Fest, Dayton. Mission Mountain Winery, 82420 U.S. Highway 93. (406) 849-5524; www.missionmountainwinery.com. Mission Mountain serves up tastes of their annual vertical of Pinot Noir wines, including older vintages, the current release, and a barrel sample of an upcoming wine. Part educational seminar on the pairing of food and wine, there is also a large variety of sausages served.

NOVEMBER

Thanksgiving Weekend at the Winery, Dayton. Mission Mountain Winery, 82420 U.S. Highway 93. (406) 849-5524; www .missionmountainwinery.com. Thanksgiving weekend is a wonderful time for a drive around the Flathead for a little more to eat and a little more to drink. To further the love of wine and food, Mission Mountain Winery hosts a pairing of holiday foods with wines. Try smoked salmon bruschetta and Monster Chardonnay, pork loin and Riesling, meatballs in Pinot Noir wine sauce, Death by Chocolate Cake and Merlot Reserve, or Ice Wine Ginger Pear Cake. Mission Mountain Winery is located on Highway 93 in Dayton, on the west shore of beautiful Flathead Lake.

Landmark Eateries

Bojangles Diner, 1319 U.S. Highway 2 West, Kalispell; (406) 755-3222; $. Like listening to the oldies station on the radio, this

1950s-style restaurant will bring back memories. Elvis, Marilyn Monroe, and Buddy Holly are plastered on the walls and in the menu items (try the Buddy Holly burger). In addition to some of the area's best lemon meringue pie, they serve up classic burgers, fries, and milkshakes. If it's huckleberry season, order two slices of pie (one for the road), because they won't last long.

Double Front Café, 122 West Alder St., Missoula; (406) 543-6264; $$. There are no frills at this favorite locals' cowboy cafe. It's been around for decades and promises good old-fashioned comfort food when you need something to stick to your ribs. The atmosphere may be basic, but folks rave about the fried chicken.

Echo Lake Café, 1195 Highway 83, Bigfork; (406) 837-4252; www.echolakecafe.com; $$. Open since 1960, this warm cafe is on the way to some of the area's best hiking (Jewel Basin) and is a longstanding locals' favorite for breakfast and lunch. The consistently delicious food, warm woody interior, roomy booths, and friendly service from owners Bob and Christi Young keep the place bustling seven days a week. Omelets, blueberry pancakes, homemade granola, Cobb salad, BLTs—nothing beats the basics when they are done well.

Hangin' Art Gallery and Coffee House, 92555 Highway 93, Arlee; (406) 726-5005; www.hanginartgallery.com; $. A good cup of coffee, a tasty pastry: Sometimes that's all a person needs to be happy. At this roadside coffeehouse, you'll find all that (and free Wi-Fi to boot), as well as a dose of local artwork and music every Friday night. This gathering place is as much for locals as for travelers passing through Arlee en route to Flathead or Glacier or heading back to Missoula. Denny Nault just wanted a place where people could gather, meet for lunch, have a good espresso, and connect with one another. He added an emphasis on using organic and locally grown ingredients to the homemade soups, breads, and sandwiches served in the cafe. The result is a menu that nourishes the soul as much as the stomach.

Hungry Bear Steak House, 6287 Montana Highway 83, Condon; (406) 754-2240; $$. Popular with locals and tourists who pass through on Highway 83, a scenic route to Glacier Park, the Hungry Bear is exactly 1 hour and 30 minutes from both Missoula and Kalispell. Try the Panda Bear (filet wrapped in bacon, smothered in mushrooms) or order from the "Cub Menu" for the kids. Hikers, horsemen, anglers, and visitors stop by this roadside cafe and find a comfortable, classic Montana menu.

Lake City Bakery and Eatery, 10 Second Ave. East, Polson; (406) 883-5667; $. All the breads, rolls, and sweets made here send an irresistible aroma wafting down the street. Located in a 1930s brick building that was once the Red and White Grocery, this small-town diner has a big-time view, looking out toward Flathead Lake. Lake City serves a mean breakfast and is a local favorite. Soup and bread options change daily.

La Provence, 408 Bridge St., Bigfork; (406) 837-2923; www.big forklaprovence.com; $$$. This is the restaurant with the line out on the sidewalk in the summer, and not because the service is slow. Chef Marc Guizol offers a wonderful menu typical of his native Provence, in the south of France, and has created a longstanding locals' favorite along with his wife, Caroline. This eatery has a charismatic, casual ambience that makes you want to linger for lunch on the patio over your turkey and Brie sandwich on a housemade baguette or stay for a decadent dinner. For a hearty entree with finesse, look for Cheuvreil Roti aux Figues, venison tenderloin with confit Black Mission figs and Bordeaux sauce. The couple has also crafted an excellent wine list, which earned them *Wine Spectator* magazine's top award in 2002.

Flathead Cherry Clafouti

**Approximately 30 fresh Flathead cherries,
  pitted and marinated in Chambord
  (at least 24 hours in advance)**

2 cups heavy cream

7 eggs

1 cup sugar

1 teaspoon vanilla extract

Powered sugar, for dusting

Vanilla ice cream (optional)

La Provence
408 Bridge St., Bigfork
(406) 837-2923
www.bigforklaprovence.com

1. Preheat oven to 350°F.
2. Butter six individual ovenproof brûlée dishes and place 4 or 5 marinated cherries in each dish. Set them aside.
3. In a large mixing bowl, blend the cream, eggs, sugar, and vanilla with a wire whisk. Pour the mixture evenly into each baking dish with the cherries, and place in oven. Cook until clafouti is just set and the cherries have just begun releasing their juices on the surface.
4. Allow to cool slightly, dust with powdered sugar, top with vanilla ice cream, and serve warm.

Serves 6.

The Libby Café, 411 Mineral Ave., Libby; (406) 293-3523; $. The breakfasts and lunches served here are as legendary as this town's far-north logging history. Big omelets and burgers that would feed a family are the showy staples on the menu, but there are plenty of

Queen of Muffins

From the archives of the Libby Café kitchen comes this unusual muffin recipe, taken from an 1896 cookbook by Fannie Merritt Farmer:

This is a good basic muffin recipe. You can add raisins or nuts or vary it however you wish. Happy baking.

¼ **cup butter**
½ **cup milk (scant)**
⅓ **cup sugar**
1½ **cups flour**
1 **egg**
2½ **teaspoons baking powder**

> **The Libby Café**
> **411 Mineral Ave., Libby**
> **(406) 293-3523**

1. Preheat oven to 400°F.
2. With an electric mixer, cream the butter; add sugar and well beaten egg; sift baking powder with flour, fold into the first mixture, one cup at a time, alternating with milk.
3. Bake in buttered tin gem pans or small muffin pans for 25 minutes.

Makes 1 dozen small muffins.

normal items to order, too. Hands down, it is hard to refuse the house-made Huckleberry Swirls—basically sticky buns with wild huckleberries between the layers. There are also the Huckleberry Flapjacks—sweeter than a pancake and lighter than a crepe, but sooo good! And the muffins are so wonderful that the Libby Café gals started a mail-order business over the Internet (www.montanamuffins.com), peddling muffins (of course!), cinnamon rolls, homemade huckleberry syrup, and a muffin of the month club. But I suggest you experience the home-baked goodness for yourself at the cafe.

NO. Not that great.

The Montana Club, 2620 Brooks St., Missoula; (406) 543-3200. 4561 North Reserve St., Butte; (406) 541-8141; www.montanaclub.com; $$$. The name and this quotation from the Web site say it all about this Missoula standout (now with a location in Butte, too!): "The idea was a simple one, to provide friendly down-to-earth service, portions so big there's something left over for a midnight snack, and to serve it all up in a cozy lodge-like atmosphere." This is a somewhat glitzed-up supper club and steak house (read: there's a casino next to the restaurant), but it's still approachable enough that it doesn't feel like it's a special-occasion-only place. After twenty years of serving up great steaks, this is a local tradition.

Moose's Saloon, 173 North Main St., Kalispell; (406) 755-2337; www.moosessaloon.com; $. It's nothing fancy, but the pizza is memorable and the bar has been a town staple since 1957. If these walls could talk, they would pine for the early days when Moose and Shirley Miller fixed the place up to feel like a real Montana bar. Today the swinging saloon doors open and close to the steady flow of locals and tourists alike.

Park Café, 3147 Highway 89, St. Mary; (406) 732-4482; www.parkcafe .us; $. Any restaurant with the motto "Pies for Strength" is my kind of place. And Kathryn Hiestand-Miller knows how to serve up the pie—strawberry-rhubarb, razzleberry, classic apple, banana

cream, chocolate, peach, blueberry, blackberry, huckleberry, and cherry! Since 1981, Kathryn and her husband, Neal Miller, have been cooking up great food for travelers. There are other things on the menu, from burgers to borscht, enough to satisfy the thousands of tourists who pass through the east side of Glacier National Park along the Going to the Sun Road. But the journey is only complete once they've stopped for pie at Park Café.

Expensive

Pearl Street Café and Bakery, 231 East Front St., Missoula; (406) 541-0231; www.pearlcafe.us; $$$. All-white tablecloths, wooden bistro chairs, sparkling crystal glasses, and silver flatware by the glow of firelight—it's no wonder that owner Pearl Cash's motto is "country fare with city flair." She combines urban sophistication with delicate rusticity in her menu, meaning she lets food be food, preparing it only to the point where the flavors reach their peak. After time spent in France and other epicurean endeavors, Pearl returned to Montana (she's a fourth-generation native). Her latest restaurant incarnation opened in 2004; it's just the right size, with just the right style and mix of French, American, and nouvelle flavors.

Park Café Pie Crust

½ cup flour
¼ teaspoon salt
¼ teaspoon apple cider vinegar

1 egg yolk, beaten
2 tablespoons canola oil
About 1 tablespoon water

1. Gently combine all the ingredients except the water until dough begins to form. Add just enough water to hold dough together.
2. Roll out on a pastry cloth or very lightly floured surface until dough is about 2 inches larger than pan dimensions. Ease the dough into the pan and firm into place. Trim excess with a knife or kitchen scissors.

Makes a single crust for a 9-inch pie.

Park Café
3147 Highway 89, St. Mary
(406) 732-4482
www.parkcafe.us

 Point of Rocks, 10035 Highway 93 North, mile marker 154, Olney; (406) 881-2752; $$. As you head toward the Canadian border on Highway 93 north of Whitefish, you pass blink-and-you-might-miss-it Olney. (Take your passport in case you feel like hopping over the line!) Point of Rocks is a road trip

Park Café Classic Apple Pie

2¼ pounds Golden Delicious
apples, peeled and sliced
½ cup sugar (brown sugar can
be substituted)
1 tablespoon cornstarch
1 teaspoon cinnamon

Prepared pie crust, uncooked
¼ cup (½ stick) butter, chilled
⅓ cup brown sugar
½ cup flour

1. Preheat oven to 350°F.
2. Gently toss apple slices with sugar, cornstarch, and cinnamon.
   Place apples into the prepared crust.
3. For crumble topping, mix butter, brown sugar, and flour and
   crumble with a pastry cutter or hands to get the mixture into small
   bits. Spread over the apples carefully. Lightly press topping into
   apples.
4. For perfectly cooked apples, bake the pie for 2 hours at 350°F with
   a large stainless steel bowl over the top, not touching the pie. For
   the last 10 minutes, remove the bowl, turn the oven up to 375°F,
   and brown the topping.

institution for locals. The menu is full of great basics: steak,
chicken, shrimp. Dinners are served with soup and salad; choice of
baked potato, fries, steak fries, or rice; cheese toast; and house
dessert. The cheese toast is one of those things you will crave and
return for time after time.

Polebridge Mercantile and Cabins, 265 Polebridge Loop, Polebridge; (406) 888-5105; $$. Most people stumble upon this little bakery on a dirt road in the middle of nowhere. They find it looking for a restroom or stopping to ask for directions on the way to hike or camp around Kintla Peak in the Waterton-Glacier International Peace Park or to fish the North Fork of the Flathead River. But the aroma of baking bread, cinnamon rolls, and (if you are lucky) huckleberry macaroons leads them into the mercantile and makes them stay. The setting is so remote, so unique and enchanting, that the Polebridge Merc is a destination in itself. Built in 1914, it was a pioneer store on the edge of Glacier just a few years after the national park was established. It remains the same—part general store, and part last outpost of civilization, where owners Deb and Dan Kaufman serve a really good cup of coffee and fabulous pastries.

The Raven Grill, 25999 Montana Highway 35, Bigfork; (406) 837-2836; $$. Nothing says summer on Flathead Lake like a drink and dinner at the Raven (although it is open year-round; ask about the annual New Year's Day Polar Plunge), sitting on the dock as the sun goes down on the opposite side of the lake. The food ranges from "Margarita and Mexican" on Mondays to Sushi Saturdays, and toss in the Caribbean calamari or classic pad Thai.

The Red Bird Restaurant and Wine Bar, 111 North Higgins, Missoula; (406) 549-2906; www.redbirdrestaurant.com; $$$. Falling somewhere between a French bistro and a Spanish tapas bar, with an international flair, Red Bird presents small works of art on every plate. Husband and wife team Jim Tracey and Laura Waters opened their doors in November 1996 with a mission to provide Missoula with innovative cuisine using fresh local ingredients. Folded into the lobby of the historic Florence Hotel, it has the charm of an old-world cafe with a very contemporary menu that changes seasonally (and nightly, if you count specials). A staple appetizer is the house-made sausage, which changes weekly; the grilled bison tenderloin drizzled with truffle oil is also mouthwateringly good.

Red's Wines & Blues, 30 2nd St. East, Kalispell; (406) 755-9463; $$$. This is Kalispell's hippest hangout when it comes to food and wine. Open since 2004, but set in a remodeled historic building, utilizing the naturally interesting exposed brick walls and antique pressed-tin ceilings, it has the atmosphere of a gussied-up saloon. The menu is varied and emphasizes local greens and meats. You can never go wrong with a steak in Montana, and the New York strip is a great choice at this place.

River City Grill, 7985 Montana Highway 200, Bonner; (406) 258-2758; $$. The historic Western Lumber Company building was converted to a restaurant in 1997. That it

was meant to cater to anglers coming off the Blackfoot River is clear based on the fact that they serve breakfast until 2 p.m. every day. The menu is all comfort food, homespun and filling, hence the signature cream of tomato soup and homemade pies. But Friday and Saturday nights the place is packed for the prime rib and shrimp dinners. My favorite is the buffalo burger with sweet potato fries and chipotle mayo dressing.

Showthyme, 548 Electric Ave., Bigfork; (406) 837-0707; www .showthyme.com; $$. If you are a "Life is short, eat dessert first" type of person, then owners Rose and Blu Funk know you will love their housemade ice cream. Order the vertical banana split, huckle-berry crepes filled with huckleberry ice cream and topped with huckleberry sauce and a sampling of the flavors du jour. But really, as your mom always said, you should eat your dinner—you won't be disappointed. Blu does most of the cooking and combines French, Thai, and Italian influences in a menu that emphasizes steaks and seafood. Located next to the "off Broadway" theater, the restaurant fills up quickly before a play, hence the name.

Stevie Café, 202 Main St., Stevensville; (406) 777-2171; $$. Several years back, Stevie Café renovated the adjacent Old Corner Bar into a restaurant for lunch and dinner, so what was once a popular coffee spot has become one of the town's most popular eateries. It serves up delicious classic Montana fare (read: steak) and the historic location is memorable.

The Stray Bullet, 403 Main St., Ovando; (406) 793-4030; $. This cafe doesn't need to advertise. Located on remote Highway 200, the hundred-year-old building with a high false front can be seen for miles before you smell the coffee brewing. The place is named for a bullet lodged in the wall, remnant of a late 1800s gun fight. (The angle of the shot shows it to have come from a bar that used to be where the Ovando post office is now.) The restaurant is a soup and sandwich shop with an espresso bar, visited by anglers who frequent the Blackfoot River. It's sort of a last outpost in the wilderness (the Bob Marshall Wilderness is across the road): Ovando is described by Meriwether Lewis in his journals, though he likely wasn't able to order a triple half-caf skinny iced latte.

Tiebuckers Pub and Eatery, 75 Somers Rd., Somers; (406) 857-3335; $$. The best part about Tiebuckers is the feeling of discovery you get when you turn off busy Highway 35 onto this country road. Around one bend you are greeted with this off-the-beaten-path restaurant (the building is a converted and remodeled railroad depot) with its garden paths that beckon you in. Owners Julie and Barry Smith work the restaurant regularly to ensure a wonderful consistency in the food and service; everyone who walks in is made to feel like a regular. The menu is typical seafood, steaks, ribs, and pasta. I like a good ol' cheeseburger and local microbrew on tap in the pub.

Triple Creek Ranch, 5551 West Fork Rd., Darby; (406) 821-4600; www.triplecreekranch.com; $$$$. This is an elegantly rustic resort, meaning that the setting is in the middle of nowhere (views of the Bitterroot Mountains abound) but the cabins are posh and the food is wildly delicious. Executive chef Jacob Leatherman concocts epicurean dishes that you don't see on just any menu in Montana: Pan-Seared Skate Wing with a Salsifed Puree or Pheasant Confit and Field Greens with a Pear and White Truffle Vinaigrette. His menu features high-concept fare that he perfected at the Home Ranch, a resort in Clark, Colorado.

HISTORIC HOTELS OF GLACIER

Glacier National Park's steep mountain terrain inspired a Swiss Alps architectural style for the historic buildings that ornament the countryside. Each hotel is a wonderful place to stay and dine, if not just for the views, then for the thoughtful menus offered at each place.

Belton Chalet, 12575 Highway 2 East, West Glacier; (406) 888-5000; www.beltonchalet.com; $$$. Built in 1910 and impeccably restored in 2000 by Cas Still and Andy Baxter, the Belton Chalet is a jewel in the "Crown of the Continent" national park—and the restaurant is another gem. The hotel's roots go back to the early days when the Great Northern Railway championed passenger trains into the mountains of the park for tourists (an Amtrak sleeper still runs past here from Seattle). The restaurant was the height of luxury at the time and retains the same elegance today. Most guests see the chalet during the summer months, and fewer in the autumn, but the best time to visit is winter, when the snow blankets everything in quiet. The Going to the Sun Road

Triple Creek's exclusive service has created interest in a chef's table, where guests can observe a multicourse meal in all stages of preparation. A 2000-bottle wine room that features vintages from around the world, perfect for sipping in the fireside lounge.

Tupelo Grille and Fine Wine, 17 Central Ave., Whitefish; (406) 862-6146; www.tupelogrille.com; $$. Set in the tiny burg of Whitefish since 1995, Tupelo doesn't have a single visitor who

is closed, but cross-country skiing beckons, as does the decadent Sunday brunch menu with the Farmhouse Breakfast Bake or Elk Sirloin and Poached Eggs. Dinner is equally as hearty (weekends only during winter), and in warmer months it's wonderful to begin with cocktails on the deck (tremendous views), then move into the dining room for classic continental cuisine.

Izaak Walton Inn, 290 Izaak Walton Inn Rd., Essex; (406) 888-5700; www.izaakwaltoninn.com; $$$. From Browning, you'll continue to the eastern edge of Glacier National Park and Essex, home to the historic Izaak Walton Inn. Listed on the National Register of Historic Places, the Izaak Walton is an alpine lodge constructed in 1939 by the Great Northern Railroad to house winter snow removal crews. Today it seems more glamorous than that: Nostalgia lingers in the hotel and in the restaurant. Comfort food is served up with "Montana signature" ingredients, including wild huckleberries, top-notch beef, quality buffalo meats, Rocky Mountain elk, and rainbow trout. The Dining Car Restaurant is adorned with railroad memorabilia that showcases Glacier's history

continued on next page

continued from previous page

with the Great Northern Railroad. Open year-round, it's a unique experience that tops off any visit to the national park.

Glacier Park Lodge, Glacier National Park; (406) 756-2444; www.glacierparkinc.com; $$$. This remarkable log structure was built in 1913 by the Great Northern Railway. The immense Douglas fir columns that support the lodge span three stories up a central colonnade in the lobby. Staying and dining here is all about that first impression when you walk into the lobby's vaulted ceilinged grandeur. At the Great Northern Steak and Rib House the food can be unremarkable with standard steaks and shrimp fare, but the overall experience of history and setting will be memorable.

Lake McDonald Lodge, Glacier National Park; (406) 892-2525 or (406) 888-5431; www.glacierparkinc.com; $$$. Cowboy artist C. M. Russell built his cabin and painting studio on the shores of Lake McDonald. He frequented the saloon in Apgar, and

doesn't rave. A Georgian guest says the grits are better than those in most places in the South. The place specializes in Cajun and Southern cuisine, mostly in the form of fresh seafood. This is not just dirty rice and gumbo; look for creative original items like the spicy Shrimp Cambas Pil Pil (gulf shrimp sautéed in chile oil with garlic and parsley) and expect to get your fingers fantastically greasy. For the neater eaters, don't pass up the Looziana Crawfish Cakes with tarragon mustard aioli.

in many ways his fireside stories, as much as his art, still live on throughout the park. Appropriately, hunting trophies and rough-hewn Western red cedar beams in Russell's Fireside Dining Room at the historic Lake McDonald Lodge recall the building's hunting lodge origins. The dinner menu leans toward wild game but is varied for other tastes.

Many Glacier Hotel, Glacier National Park; (406) 892-2525 or (406) 732-4411; www.glacierparkinc.com; $$$. Picture windows frame views of Many Glacier's impressive peaks, inspiring the Swiss Alps atmosphere of the hotel and the Ptarmigan Dining Room. Dining here is mostly about the views and ambience; the menu offers continental and American cuisine. The highlight of eating at Many Glacier is the Interlaken Lounge, which offers Après Fondue daily from 2 p.m. to 4 p.m. Who doesn't like fondue? The flavorful Four Cheese Fondue and mouthwatering Montana-Made Chocolate Fondue will make a stay unforgettable.

Victor Steakhouse & Lounge, 2426 Meridian Rd., Victor; (406) 642-3300; $$. Paper napkins along with the crackers and cheese starter are hallmarks of this classic Montana supper club: nothing fancy, just great steaks and ultra-friendly people. In a farm community of fewer than 1,000 residents, this is the place to have a nice meal and catch up with the "neighbors."

The Whistlestop Café at Station 8, 1024 U.S. Highway 49, East Glacier; (406) 226-9292; $$. This is a little log cabin with a diner menu and the friendly service to match. It may be the only place that serves baked oatmeal in Montana. For a breakfast that tastes a lot like a dessert, there's also the stuffed huckleberry French toast. (For the real thing, just order the huckleberry pie, available any time.) Heartier specialties include barbecue pork and tender ribs.

Brewpubs & Microbreweries

Bayern Brewing, 1507 Montana St., Missoula; (406) 721-1482; www.bayernbrewery.com. Montana's oldest brewing company (since 1987) serves up some of the smoothest brews in the business—the Bayern Amber, with a smooth hoppy taste, is a perennial favorite. Owner and brewmaster Jürgen Knöller is a German Diploma Master Brewer. He began brewing in 1978 at age sixteen and endured rigorous training in Germany, which gives him the right to claim to be the state's only German brewery (and arguably the only one in the Rocky Mountains). The taproom is open year-round, serving up six beers regularly, and the beer garden (music included) is open from April through October. Call for reservations if you'd like a tour of the brewery. Look for award-winning Bayern beers in grocery stores all over Montana: The Dragon's Breath Dark Hefeweizen was recently released in six-packs and the wheaty Dancing Trout sold 1 million

Look this place up. They're unique.

bottles in 2009, with some of the proceeds benefiting the Trout Unlimited chapter in Missoula.

Big Sky Brewing, 5417 Trumpeter Way, Missoula; (406) 549-2777; www.bigskybrew .com. With labels that are cleverly irreverent and eye-catching—Trout Slayer Ale, Moose Drool Brown Ale, Scape Goat Pale Ale, and Powder Hound Winter Ale among them—Big Sky brews have surged across the West. It helps that they taste great, too. The Moose Drool is earthier than its amber equivalent but perfectly balanced for the average Joe microbrew palate. The company started brewing English-inspired ales in 1995, selling only draft. Now the beers are available by the bottle, can, and keg, to the tune of over 38,000 barrels per year. A visit to the taproom with a tour of the brewery and bottling line is worthwhile; you can fill growlers and buy Big Sky Brewing stuff.

Bitterroot Brewing Company, 101 Marcus St., Hamilton; (406) 363-PINT (7468); www.bitterrootbrewing.com. Montana-grown and Montana-malted barley is the base for all of the beers at this local pub. The classic six handcrafted brews—Sawtooth, Nut Brown, Pale, Porter, Amber, and IPA—are always on tap here, along with seasonal beers and what they call "brewer's whims." If you are fortunate enough to catch these whim-taps, try Huckleberry Hefeweizen, an unfiltered wheat beer with natural huckleberry flavor, or Zaxan

Coffee Milk Stout, which uses local roasted beans and lots of milk and sugar for a sweet finish.

Blacksmith Brewing Company, 114 Main St., Stevensville; (406) 777-0680; www.blacksmithbrewing.com. You won't find Blacksmith Brewing Company beers on the shelves of the local grocery store. There's no bottling line or distribution channel for their product: This small brewer sells everything it brews on tap at the pub and that's the way they like it—local. Co-owners Eric Hayes and Pamela Kaye reclaimed a dilapidated 1907 brick building that once served as the town's blacksmith shop and opened the brewery in 2008. Developing a casual, approachable atmosphere, plus a straightforward line of microbrews with brewmaster Mike Howard, the crew has hit on a perfect formula for small-town living. Featuring five regular pours, including the BrickHouse Blonde, an American-style Hefeweizen, that according to Howard is a "transition" beer for Budweiser drinkers trying to get their mouths around handcrafted brews. Howard also added a dry-hopped Cutthroat IPA for the "hopheads" and a traditional robust Pulaski Porter with its rich maltiness for those cold winter nights. The brewer features live music regularly and the friendly scene is made all the better in the historic surroundings.

 Flathead Lake Brewing, 26008 East Lake Shore Dr., Bigfork; (406) 222-7837; www.flatheadlakebrewing.com. In 2008, Flathead Lake Brewing won the People's Choice Award at the Montana Beer Festival with one of its seasonal brews, Rising Sun Espresso Porter.

And it's no wonder—this is a "people's" kind of pub—laid back, small, and easy to like. Brewmeister and owner Terry Leonard seems to be in the business purely for the love of his craft, making only small batches in this brewery on a sliver of land along Highway 35 (at mile marker 26) in Woods Bay, across from the Islander Inn.

Glacier Brewing Company, 6 10th Ave. East, Polson; (406) 883-2595; www.glacierbrewing.com. The first thing I noted about all the Glacier Brewing Company's ales is the remarkable clarity in the color, even in the darkest Slurry Bomber Stout—it must be the water. Dave Ayers, owner and brewer, humbly claims it's just the process he uses. He'll give you a free tour of the brewery and pour a draft of whatever is on tap. Brewing six fine handcrafted beers on the premises, plus a line of nonalcoholic sodas, this little joint has a casual taproom and a beer garden out back. Push through the swinging saloon doors of the taproom, belly up to the bar for a brew, and bring the kids along for a soda and an earful of good stories from the barkeep.

 Great Northern Brewing, 2 Central Ave., Whitefish; (406) 863-1000; www.greatnorthernbrewing.com. You can't miss the Great Northern Brewing building on a prime corner in tiny Whitefish. Three glassed-in stories house the "gravity flow" system and this town gathering place. Started by Minott Wessinger, the great-great-grandson of Henry Weinhard, the Great Northern Brewing Company was built in 1994 to brew Black Star Golden Lager. The brewery no longer brews Black Star beer, but it does brew eleven various styles of craft beer. Best known is the American-style Hefe, Wheatfish, crisp, light, and extremely drinkable (too much so!). The brewery offers two daily tours of the brewing facilities from Monday through Friday.

Kettlehouse Brewing Company, 602 Myrtle St., Missoula; (406) 728-1660; www.kettlehouse.com. Producing consistent award-winning beers at the North American Brewers Association brewfests, Kettlehouse is able to offer a wide array of brews (some served only in the taproom) without compromising quality. The locals' fave is the Cold Smoke Scotch Ale, which won gold medals at NABA in 2009. If you visit the new taproom on Missoula's north side, you might be lucky enough to sample the Bong Water Porter (if it's legal by then) or settle for any of the other handcrafted K-hole (the local nickname) ales made from Montana malted barley.

Coldsmoke [handwritten annotation]

Tamarack Brewing Company Alehouse and Grill, 105 Blacktail Rd., Lakeside; (406) 844-0244; www.tamarackbrewing .com. This casual brewpub is situated near the turnoff for Blacktail Mountain ski area and on the west side of Flathead, keeping up a lively clientele regardless of the season. From your seat in this contemporary-hip restaurant you can watch the entire brewing process. Craig Koontz brews Tamarack's own line of ales, which range from Bear Bottom Blonde Kolsch Ale to the rich Old Stache Porter. The alehouse also serves up other Montana microbrews from as close as Flathead Lake Brewing Company, its eastern neighbor, to as far as Belt (in the central section of the state) and many taps beyond. This is a great hangout spot.

Most of the state being more suitable to wheat, barley, and cattle, Montana is not known for wine. Yet the state's western region yields a burgeoning culture of winemakers and vineyards. Although the western region of the state borders Idaho, which earned a 2007 designation as "the new frontier of wine country" through the American Viticulture Area, Montana vineyards have not received much attention. There are a handful of winemakers producing good wine in this region and only a few who grow and make their own vintages, but perhaps the future will bring a culture of wine.

Vineyards pepper the area, according to the Montana Winegrowers Institute: Some properties are dedicated to growing Pinot Noir and other varieties on Finley Point. Partridge Hill Vineyard on Sunnyslope, northwest of Polson, is growing a variety of clones of Pinot Noir and experimenting with many other varieties, such as Pinot Gris, Chardonnay, and Merlot. Gregor Tavenner has taken over the old Walker experimental vineyard and added some exciting new plantings of Pinot Noir and Pinot Gris above the eastern shores of Flathead Lake north of Finley Point. Hartman Vineyard recently planted Pinot Noir vines next to an old apricot orchard near Yellow Bay; Gewürztraminer and Pinot Noir grow in Moise; and the Simonsen family farm is growing Gewürztraminer between Plains and Thompson Falls. Additionally, some resourceful fruit growers make memorable fruit wines, ranging from Flathead cherry to elderberry flavors, preserving a homespun tradition.

Whatever the fruit, let your palate lead the way through Montana wine country. The next frontier?

Flathead Lake Winery, 29 Golden Eagle St., Columbia Falls; (406) 387-WINO (9466); www.flatheadlakewinery.com. Owner and winemaker Paddy Fleming is a fifth-generation Montanan whose ancestors were some of the first pioneers in the state. The Diamond F logo that appears on the wine labels is actually the state certified brand that marks livestock registered to Fleming's family ranch. Living off the land, so to speak, led the Flemings to make their own fruit wine for family and friends. In 2003 they started making wines for the commercial market, using 100 percent Montana fruits and doing all the bottling and corking themselves. Flathead Lake Winery is known for small-batch wines of crisp sweetness, from the Gewürztraminer to the white cherry. The wines are available in grocery and specialty markets throughout Montana. The tasting room is located in Polebridge, on the western border of Glacier National Park; call for reservations and directions.

Hidden Legend Winery, 1345 U.S. Highway 93 North #5, Victor; (406) 363-MEAD (6323); www.hiddenlegendwinery.com. The indescribable taste of mead—heavy, honeyed, warming—is a revived art at Hidden Legend Winery (formerly Trapper Creek Winery), where the winemaker's results sit somewhere between dry grape wines and traditional meads. Technically made from fermented honey, these meads are much more sophisticated; meadmaker Ken Schultz currently makes six varieties, including a dark honey mead, a spiced mead, and huckleberry and chokecherry meads. Tour the meadery and experience mead from start to finish from Tuesday through Friday, 11 a.m. to 6 p.m., and Saturday, 11 a.m. to 8:30 p.m.

Lolo Peak Winery, 2506 Mount Ave., Missoula; (406) 549-1111; www.lolopeak.com. Judy Chapman has made a hobby into a profession by using fruit and honey wine recipes from her father and crafting a burgeoning business. Since 1997 she has captured the flavor of Montana summer in a bottle. She uses seasonal fruits of the region, including Flathead cherries, Bitterroot Valley apples, Mission Valley raspberries, Frenchtown-area plums, and rhubarb from Missoula-area gardens. Stop by to taste the wide range of sweet, fruity beverages. The tasting room is open from Monday through Saturday, 10 a.m. to 6 p.m.

Mission Mountain Winery, 82420 U.S. Highway 93, Dayton; (406) 849-5524; www.missionmountainwinery.com. Montana's first winery (since 1984) was started by Dr. Tom Campbell Jr. and his father, Tom Campbell Sr. Young Tom is a UC Davis–trained winemaker who worked for Ste. Michelle in California and Quail Run (now Covey Run) in Washington before starting his own vineyard on the shores of Flathead Lake.

The winery currently produces approximately 6,500 cases of wine a year. The wines produced include Vin Gris, Riesling, Monster Chardonnay, Pinot Gris, Gewürztraminer, a "blush" wine called Sundown, an exceptional Muscat Canelli dinner wine, Nouveaux Riche, a dessert Muscat Canelli, Ice Wine, Cabernet Sauvignon,

Merlot, Pinot Noir, Monster Red, a Merlot-Cabernet blend, Syrah, Cream Sherry, Port, Cocoa Vin (a chocolate Port), and Blanc de Noir Champagne. But of these small-batch wines, the repeated award-winner is Mission Mountain's Riesling, made from a blend of grapes out of Washington, Idaho, and Montana.

Besides having one of the most beautiful settings for a winery, looking across Flathead Lake and toward the Mission Mountain Range to the east, Dr. Tom Jr. has also been a pioneer of cold-hardy grape varietals that flourish in this banana belt where the growing season lasts from May through October before temperatures drop to freezing. The tasting room is open daily from May through October, 10 a.m. to 5 p.m.

Ten Spoon Vineyard and Winery, 4175 Rattlesnake Dr., Rattlesnake Valley; (406) 549-8703; www.tenspoonwinery .com. Making its mark on local palates as well as the national stage, in 2009 Ten Spoon Winery was awarded gold, silver, and bronze medals for its Range Rider, Prairie Thunder, St. Pepin, and Paradise Pear at the Northwest Wine Summit. Using all organic Montana-grown grapes with no added sulfites, Ten Spoon has forged a new respect for Montana wineries since it began officially selling wines in 2003. Situated on the edge of the Rattlesnake Wilderness (northeast of Missoula), the vineyard's growing season is short, but the days are long from May to October and have yielded a surprising bounty of interesting crops.

They grow several cold-hardy varietals: Maréchal Foche, Frontenac, Leon Millot, St. Croix, and table grape Swenson Red (reds) and St. Pepin and LaCrosse (whites). From the harvest—an all-time high of 14 tons in October 2008—comes Ranger Rider, Farm Dog, and St. Pepin (formerly Fat Cat). There is no tasting room at Ten Spoon Vineyard, but the wines are widely available all over the state, as well as in Washington, Oregon, and Wyoming. Look for the National Park wines on your travels through Glacier and Yellowstone.

Trapper Peak Winery, 75 Cattail Ln., Darby; (406) 821-1964; www.trapperpeakwinery.com. Founded in 2002 by Keith and Tonia Smith, Trapper Peak Winery is backed with twenty years of agricultural experience in the Bitterroot Valley. The couple started planting acres of hayfield with grapes, year by year, until all 106 acres of productive land had become a vineyard. And they are not shy about choosing to produce the big reds: Cabernet, Merlot, and Petite Sirah. But what's most likely to be found on any dinner table is the American Rodeo Red, a unique blend of Cabernet Sauvignon,

Petite Sirah, and Zinfandel grapes. Look for it in grocery stores and on restaurant wine lists throughout western Montana. No vineyard tours.

Learn to Cook

Flathead Valley Community College, 777 Grandview Dr., Kalispell; (406) 756-3822; www.fvcc.edu. This growing Professional Chef/Hospitality Management program is designed to train students for the demands of a professional restaurant kitchen and a management level in the hospitality industry. But this two-year program also has an eye on the little things, such as maintaining local connections with an expanded "Farm-to-Table" initiative, teaching students to take advantage of cooking with meat and produce from local gardens, farms, and ranches. That means students can learn the benefits of dehydrating fresh fruit or the art of canning and preserving produce right alongside ice sculpture lessons in a showcase commercial-quality teaching kitchen. Continuing education and evening classes are available for nondegree students.

aka Missoula College

University of Montana College of Technology, 3639 South Ave. West, Missoula; (406) 243-7831; www.cte.umt.edu. From classes on the art of bread baking to knife skills, this two-year accredited college can prepare anyone for the demands of a commercial kitchen. Night courses and summer sessions are available for degree-seeking students or for the home cook looking to hone some of the finer points of his or her culinary repetoire.

This book is a copple years old. "A

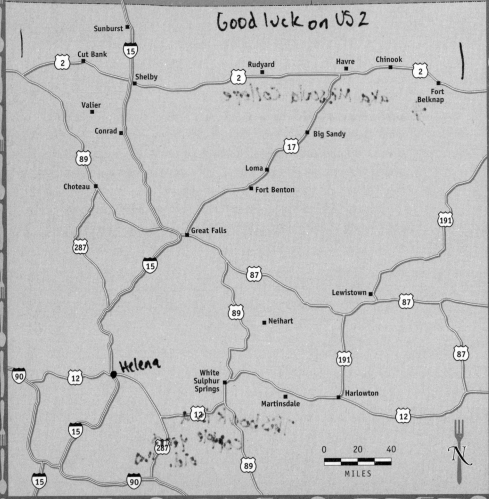

Russell Country

ALBERTA

Good luck on US 2

ave Mdescla College

Russell Country (Central)

This is land rich in resources and diverse topography. It touches every part of Montana, from the small farms that dot the lower southern portion near White Sulphur Springs and Martinsdale to the great plains of the north up near Havre and the mountain country farther to the northwest, which just touches the edge of the Continental Divide near Glacier National Park. It's no wonder famous cowboy artist C. M. Russell loved this country and memorialized it in his paintings. This is where the Native American North Fork trail tipped into America before that was its name, where bison roamed en masse, and where the open prairies sweep up into the Rocky Mountain Front.

Russell set his claim near Great Falls, which remains the center of this portion of the state even today, but the artist moved all around and explored the farthest stretches of the Missouri and Smith Rivers. The works of this colorful character now sell for millions of dollars and keep the dream of settling in the West alive in the hearts of many. Russell, like so many homesteaders before him, fell in love with this open space and the unique native culture of the land.

Other people settled around the thoroughfares of these rivers and mountains, and then settled around the railroad route, leaving a trail of towns that struggle to eke out a living yet find comfort in communities of a few hearty souls. Where those kindred folks congregate, you're sure to find some fine places to dine. While small farmers' markets and folksy food festivals abound in central Montana, restaurants are a little harder to find. But the good ones are tried and true; you won't be disappointed.

Made or Grown Here

A Land of Grass, 564 Graham Ranch Ln., Conrad; (406) 278-0159. Raising natural grass-fed beef and lamb on the family farm, the Schmidts take a little extra care because it is good for the land and good for you. Their animals are raised naturally without antibiotics or growth hormones, and they accept direct customer orders for quarters, halves, or wholes of beef between June and January. Call to find out the availability of lambs; they deliver within 200 miles of Conrad.

Elliotts of Montana, 2702 Front St., Fort Benton; (888) 622-4484; www.elliottsofmontana.com. I discovered this premade cookie dough when my daughter was selling the product for a

Amber Waves of Grain

As the seat of Pondera County, Conrad sits about an hour north of Great Falls, in the middle of Montana's Golden Triangle. The Golden Triangle covers the area from Great Falls north to Havre, then west to Cut Bank and southeast back to Great Falls. This region of north-central Montana exports more wheat than the rest of the state. Most of the agricultural land in Pondera County grows spring wheat for bread, winter wheat for noodles, and barley for beer.

fund-raiser. Elliotts products are made in a facility in Fort Benton, where they concoct mixes of brownies and twelve different kinds of cookies. The dough is made without preservatives and tastes as good as homemade without any mixing, measuring, or mess. Voilà—cookies in ten minutes!

E.T. Poultry, 7259 U.S. Highway 89, Belt; (406) 788-9901 or (406) 277-3004. Montana-raised and Montana-processed certified-organic chicken is the mainstay of this family farm, which supplies the University of Montana, along with several small grocers in the state, with fryers and roasters.

McAlpine Ranch, 1836 Bullhead Rd., Valier; (406) 667-2332; www.mopcoop.org. Clay McAlpine's family has been ranching in central Montana since 1943. After graduating from college to take over part of the family ranch, Clay realized that natural methods were better in the long run for the health of the land and his family. As a result, he employs a holistic management program for raising organic grass-fed beef and lamb. The animals are treated humanely and grow in a natural environment of fresh air, sunshine, and green pastures. The ranch uses no antibiotics, growth hormones, chemical parasiticides, or genetically modified organisms. McAlpine meats are available through the Montana Organic Producers Co-op Web site.

Timeless Foods, 120 4th Ave. Southeast, Conrad; (406) 271-5770; www.timelessfood.com. From the heart of Montana's Golden Triangle come these healthy grains, sold all over the country. Started by four organic farmers in 1993, Timeless offers premium-quality lentils, peas, flax, chickpeas, and hulless barley, and multigrain fiber nutraceutical Super BioVitality—a unique blend of Timeless organic grains, vegetable powders, and Chinese healing herbs. Like little gems in a bag, the hearty legumes are available in an array of colors from black to crimson.

Two Feathers Buffalo Jerky, 702 U.S. Highway 89 North, White Sulphur Springs; (406) 547-2240; www.brokenwillowbison.com. Bison is healthy and just as meaty as beef, with fewer calories, less cholesterol, and less fat. Broken Willow Bison Ranch in White Sulphur Springs raises bison with no growth hormones. They are fed natural hay and grasses, producing healthy, delicious meat.

Timeless Foods' Petite Crimson Lentil and Coconut Soup

The combination of coconut, chile pepper, and various spices gives this quick lentil soup the aroma and exotic flavor of India.

1 tablespoon sunflower oil

2 red onions, finely chopped

2 cloves garlic, minced

1 chile pepper, seeded and finely sliced

1-inch piece of fresh lemongrass, outer leaves removed and inside finely sliced

1 cup Timeless Petite Crimson Lentils

1 teaspoon ground coriander

1 teaspoon paprika

1⅔ cup coconut milk

3¾ cups water

Juice of 1 lime

3 scallions, chopped

1 scant cup cilantro, finely chopped

Salt and freshly ground black pepper to taste

1. Heat oil in large, deep pan. Add onions, garlic, chile pepper, and lemongrass. Cook, stirring occasionally, for 5 minutes, until onions have softened.
2. Add lentils and spices. Pour in coconut milk and water. Stir. Bring to boil, stir, then reduce to a simmer and cook for 20–30 minutes, until lentils are soft and mushy.
3. Pour in lime juice and scallions and cilantro, reserving a little of the scallions and cilantro for garnish.
4. Add salt and pepper and adjust seasoning to taste.
5. Ladle into bowls and garnish with reserved scallions and cilantro.

Serves 4.

Timeless Foods

120 4th Ave Southeast, Conrad

(406) 271-5770

www.timelessfood.com

Baker Bob's Big Stack Bakery, 112 Central Ave., Great Falls; (406) 727-5910. Baker Bob's is recommended by locals as home to the best old-time pasties this side of the divide. I'll be honest, I didn't make it to the savory part of the menu; I got stuck with a giant cinnamon roll (fresh from the oven!) and would recommend that experience to everyone.

Bear Paw Coffee Shop & Deli, 722 3rd St., Big Sandy; (406) 378-2320. Driving down from the remote north of the state's Hi-Line, where anything green often comes from a can, this place is like an oasis. Fresh spinach salad with sweet strawberries as garnish, healthy deli sandwiches, and other thoughtfully made items round out the menu. But the real centerpiece is the baking—cinnamon rolls, cakes, pastries, and delicate cookies made from family recipes are the perfect complement to a nice cappuccino in the cozy restaurant.

Big Spring Market, 613 1st Ave. South, Lewistown; (406) 708-4141. Opened in 2008, a community cooperative grocery store in a region that sports the nickame "The Golden Triangle" for agricultural production seems like a no-brainer. Located in the old Harvest States grain elevator, the market was opened by John Payne to sell organic, natural, and most importantly, fresh locally grown foods.

The Bon Ton, 312 West Main St., Lewistown; (406) 535-9650; http://bontonsodafountain.com. If you ask me, any place that touts homemade baked goods, candies, chocolates, and gifts is a place I'd like to be. But the Bon Ton is one of Lewistown's oldest businesses and it has a lovely sense of nostalgia. In 1908, the soda fountain and confectionery opened and they thrived through the Roaring 20s, the Depression, two world wars, and the good ol' days of the 50s. Even today, it's a trip down memory lane for ice cream sodas, root beer floats, and fudge.

Candy Masterpiece, 120 Central Ave., Great Falls; (406) 727-5955. Owner and chief candymaker Angie Bruskotter's motto is "Chocolate is my life!" That explains the fact that her candy shop offers thirty different kinds of fudge on any given day of the week. Bushel baskets of bulk candy, from pixie sticks to gobstoppers, line the center of the shop, but the main event is the saltwater taffy machine and the cases full of handmade truffles and fudge. This is not your grandmother's fudge, mind you; it's crazy-delicious fudge with names like Heavenly Goo and Montana Nugget and Almond Joy. You can sample them all before you buy a pound (or two) for home.

The Coffee Cup, 322 West Main St., Lewistown; (406) 535-2690. The Coffee Cup's espresso is organic, fair trade, and shade grown (both the decaf and regular)—and the service is nice, too.

Hempl's Champagne Cake

⅔ cup butter
1½ cups sugar
2¾ cups all-purpose flour
3 teaspoons baking powder
1 teaspoon salt
1 cup Champagne
6 egg whites

Hempl's Bakery
16 6th St. Southwest, Great Falls
(406) 761-3330

1. Preheat oven to 350°F. Butter a 10-inch round cake pan.
2. In a large bowl, cream together butter and sugar until very light and fluffy. Sift flour, baking powder, and salt together, and then blend into creamed mixture alternately with Champagne.
3. In a large clean bowl, beat egg whites until stiff peaks form. Fold one third of the whites into batter to lighten it, then fold in remaining egg whites. Pour into prepared pan.
4. Bake for 25 to 30 minutes, or until a toothpick inserted into the cake comes out clean.

Serves 8.

Hempl's Bakery, 16 6th St. Southwest, Great Falls; (406) 761-3330. Champagne cake, fruit pizzas, donuts. Who could resist such lovely things? At old-fashioned Hempl's, the only thing unpleasant is choosing which sweet treat to take home.

In Cahoots for Tea, 118 Central Ave., Great Falls; (406) 452-2225; www.incahootsfortea.com. Owner Pam Kohut travels the world in search of tea and its elegant accoutrements to bring to her central Montana shop. She carries over 140 varieties of loose leaf and bagged teas. The prices for teas by the ounce are reasonable and the choices are so enticing that it's hard not to leave with a tin of *something*. How about Evening in Missoula, a smooth mixture of chamomile, rose hips, raspberry leaf, peppermint, vanilla passion flowers, and strawberry leaf? Or the best seller: Montana Gold, a blend of rooibos, cinnamon, orange peel, and cloves that is full of antioxidants, according to Kohut. Tea time, anyone?

Kitch's Cheese Mart, 79490 U.S. 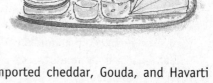 Highway 87, Lewistown; (406) 535-9770. In the least likely place (though aptly named for the collection of yard ornaments), you'll find a very nice selection of fromage. Imported cheddar, Gouda, and Havarti are all just a quick little mile-and-a-half drive west of town. You'll also find surprisingly nice choices for wines and other specialty goods here.

The Meeting Grounds, 202 North Main Ave., Choteau; (406) 466-2667. It's not that I'm just a sucker for a pun; this place really has good coffee! And there's some history to the building, too, which always adds interest to an experience. It is a 1906 bank with the vault still intact. Outside, the old lettering on the face of the brick building shows it was the Stockman State Bank.

LIVING OFF THE LAND: HUTTERITE COLONIES

At seasonal farmers' markets you may notice the distinct dress of some vendors selling produce—bearded men in white-collared shirts with black pants and vests and women in colorful long skirts or dresses with their hair covered by a scarf. These are members of the Hutterite populations that farm throughout Montana. Similar in religious beliefs to the Mennonites and the Amish, Hutterites embrace a strong separation between church and state and practice subsistence farming as a way of life. The branch of Anabaptists that we know as Hutterites was founded in Moravia in 1528 by Jacob Hutter and is distinguished from other Anabaptist sects by its belief in communal living in which all material things are held in common.

Today there are about 45,000 Hutterites living in 460 colonies, of which about 50 are in Montana. Colonies often welcome visitors and enjoy sharing glimpses of their way of life on the farm. For more information on Hutterite culture, look at www.hutterites.org.

Neihart Inconvenience Store, 316 North Main St., Neihart; (406) 236-5955. With scarcely more than a handful of home-steads and ruins of others along the 60 miles between Neihart and Great Falls on U.S. Highway 89, you have to stop at the Neihart Inconvenience Store, at the very least to find out if the folks who run it really do have a good sense of humor. They do, and they serve great pie (and espresso, too)!

Here are some of the colonies in central Montana that are open to visitors:

Ayers Colony is home to nine families and forty-two residents. It is located about 6 miles west of Grass Range, 23 miles east of Lewistown on Highway 87. Call Marilyn Stahl to arrange a visit (406-428-2207).

King Colony owns one of Montana's famous cattle ranches, King Ranch, founded in 1881. Today the farm and ranch are run by thirteen families and a total population of fifty-five people. It is located about 10 miles west of Lewistown on Highway 87 and then 2 miles north along Kolin/Ross Fork Rd. Call Rita Hofer to arrange a visit (406-538-8840).

Spring Creek Colony consists of 20,000 acres with thirteen families and a total population of forty-six people who operate a dairy farm and cattle ranch. Located 14 miles northwest of Lewistown on Highway 426, this was part of the King Ranch until it was sold in 1912. Contact resident Kathy Walter to arrange a visit (406-538-5160).

Pizazz, 403 Central Ave., Great Falls; (406) 452-6724; www .pizazzmt.com. This very chic store for masterful home cooks comes with all the gear and gadgetry of a Williams-Sonoma catalog, but tucked in between the shiny All-Clad pans, the crepe-makers, and the garlic keepers, you'll find some Montana food products. The King's Cupboard line is one, and there's a variety of regional confections. Occasionally, Pizazz offers cooking classes.

Snowy Mountain Coffee, 124 North Central, Harlowton; (406) 632-6838; www.snowymountaincoffee.com. I believe that any place that smells of freshly baked muffins when I walk through the door is a good place. At Snowy Mountain Coffee, they roast their own beans (and ship all over the world) and serve up the usual specialty coffee drinks that we've all become so addicted to. Slow Rise Bakery turns out artisanal breads, pastries, cookies, and muffins.

Farmers' Markets

Great Falls Farmers' Market, Civic Center, Great Falls. Saturday 7:45 a.m. to noon, June through September; Wednesday 4:30 p.m. to 6:30 p.m., mid-July through September.

Lewistown Farmers' Market, Symmes Park, Lewistown. Saturday 8 a.m. to noon, July through September.

Liberty County Farmers Market, Lions Park rest area, on the east side of Highway 2, Chester. Thursday 5 p.m. to 7 p.m., June through August.

S.A.T.U.R.D.A.Y. Market, Town Square, Havre. Saturday 8 a.m. to noon, July through September.

Shelby Food & Craft Farmers Market, east end of town at the city park, Shelby. Thursday 4 p.m. to 6 p.m., July through September.

MARCH

Wine and Food Festival, Great Falls; (800) 548-8256; www .bestwestern.com. When the wind howls through Great Falls in March, the food lovers celebrate with an annual Wine and Food Festival. Held at the Best Western Heritage Inn, the evening features over one hundred wines, beers to sample, and a variety of foods. Sampling begins at 6 p.m., and dancing is from 9 p.m. to midnight.

APRIL

Deliciously Decadent Dessert Social, Choteau; (406) 466-2052. Friends of the Choteau Public Library serve up the ice cream, homemade pie, or decadent dessert of your choice and coffee. The $3 ticket fee goes to support the library. From 2 p.m. to 4 p.m. at the Choteau Public Library.

JUNE

The Taste of Great Falls, Great Falls; Downtown Great Falls Association, (406) 453-6151. The Taste of Great Falls food festival challenges each restaurant to present its best dishes to the public during this exciting event. A "fair" is set up and restaurant owners offer samples of their best dishes to throngs of hungry citizens as a kickoff to summer in downtown Great Falls. Set to live music, taste diverse flavors from Cajun to sushi. This event is held in both the

Convention Center and adjacent Whittier Park. The event is from 5:00 p.m. to 9:30 p.m.

JULY

Annual Steak Fry, Choteau; (406) 466-5316. Celebrate America's independence day with some pitchfork fondued beefsteak ($12) or a Nathan, hot dog ($7), along with fresh fried potato chips, salad, baked beans, lemonade, coffee, and brownies. Hosted by the Choteau Chamber of Commerce, it's a good old-fashioned picnic with great eats. At the Pavilion from 11 a.m. to 1 p.m.

SEPTEMBER

River's Edge Trail: Blues & Brews, Great Falls; (406) 788-6197; www.thetrail.org. This event brings national blues groups together with twenty microbrews and a selection of domestic beers in Margaret Park, just north of the Mansfield Convention Center, to raise funds for the 30-mile-long River's Edge Trail that runs along the Missouri River. Thousands mass for the great fall celebration concert and foodie fest.

A food court features offerings from Great Falls restaurants, which have included shrimp cocktail, Cajun chicken, egg rolls, Gorgonzola pasta, bacon, tomato and avocado wraps, jambalaya, chopped pork sandwiches, Peruvian shrimp chowder, and chicken sausage gumbo. Desserts include carrot cake, huckleberry cheesecake, and triple-chocolate brownies. The event runs from 5:30 p.m. until midnight.

Lewistown Chokecherry Festival, Lewistown; (406) 535-5436. If you've ever popped a chokecherry in your mouth, you'll understand the genesis of this festival's kick-off event: the chokecherry pit-spitting contest. Wildly abundant, yet famously sour, bitter, and small, the chokecherry has been bringing thousands of people to Lewistown for over two decades. As much a celebration of harvest as of this prolific berry, the festival brings Main Street to life with 200 vendors who sell everything from Thai food to kettle corn, chainsaw carvings to hand-blown glass, and of course, many varieties of chokecherry jellies, syrups, wine, and treats. Other events include the Chokecherry Stomp, a dance and fund-raiser for the Community Education Center, held at the Fergus County Trade Center from 7 p.m. to midnight; carriage rides on Main Street, hosted by Half Moon Ranch; the crowning of the Chokecherry King and Queen; live music; and much more.

Liberty County Harvest Festival, Chester; (406) 759-4848; www.libertycountycc.com. Liberty County Harvest Festival is held on high school homecoming weekend, the third weekend in September. This harvest fest's highlight is the food. Locals perfect recipes for the annual chili cook-off. Prizes are awarded for Judge's Choice and People's Choice. Contestants are also encouraged to enter the pie contest and there is a cakewalk throughout the day. The event has an old-style county fair atmosphere, with plenty of craft vendors as well as game booths and food booths. Chester-Joplin-Inverness school in Chester. Saturday, 10:00 a.m. to 4:00 p.m.

Chokecherry Pie and Never-Fail Piecrust

Recipes from the Nashua Lions Club Cookbook.

Piecrust	Pie
2½ cups flour	2 tablespoons cornstarch
1 cup shortening	Small pinch of salt
1 egg, slightly beaten	2 cups chokecherry juice
1 tablespoon white vinegar	1 cup sugar
4 tablespoons water	½ teaspoon almond extract
1 teaspoon salt	1 9-inch baked pie shell (prebake at 350°F for 30 minutes until light golden brown)

Never-Fail Piecrust

1. Mix together flour and shortening until crumbly, forming pieces the size of a pea.
2. Add egg, vinegar, water, and salt. Mix well.
3. Put on floured board and roll out to fit 9-inch pie pan.

Makes 2 crusts.

Chokecherry Pie

1. Combine ingredients in a medium saucepan and cook until thick, stirring constantly. Cool.
2. Pour into baked pie shell and chill. Serve with whipped cream.

THE CHARLIE RUSSELL CHEW CHOO DINNER TRAIN

Cowboy artist C.M. Russell never ate so well in his day, but you can enjoy a hearty prime rib dinner and the entertaining train ride from Lewistown to Denton. The trip passes through rolling farmland and prairie, crossing three historic trestles and a half-mile-long tunnel on a vintage passenger train. It's a great adventure for history and train buffs and a fantastic way to illustrate a bygone era for children. The train chugs along the route of the old Chicago, Milwaukee, St. Paul, and Pacific Railroad to Denton and back again, along a spur track that was built in 1912–13 to connect Lewistown and Great Falls. Weekend voyages and special holiday Polar Run trips (with cookies, cocoa, and a visit from Santa) are scheduled throughout the year.

For tickets and more information, contact the Lewistown Chamber of Commerce at 408 Northeast Main St., Lewistown, MT 59457; (866) 912-3980 or (406) 535-5436; www .montanacharlierussellchewchoo.com.

 **Black Diamond Supper Club,** 64 Castner St., Belt; (406) 277-4118; $$. Catering to miners when it opened in 1908 as the Black Diamond Café, this restaurant has its original tin ceiling as the last sign of the building's history. Listed on the National Historical Register and situated on the Lewis and Clark Expedition Trail, the Black Diamond is most often frequented by sportsmen these days. Prime rib Saturday nights make it worth a visit.

The Breaks Ale House and Grill, 202 2nd Ave South # 5, Great Falls; (406) 453-5980; www.thebreaksgrill.com; $$. All that is trendy and hip takes place at The Breaks—microbrews, contemporary decor, and a very fancy menu. Consistently voted "Best Burger in the City," the meat here is from a ranch in Highwood where the Malek family raises certified Angus cattle. It makes a pretty fine meal, I'd say, especially mixed with black truffle oil and topped with Gorgonzola cheese!

Dante's Creative Cuisine, 1325 8th Ave. North, Great Falls; (406) 453-9599; $$$. Comfortably upscale, Dante's is in a 1908 ironworks building. Beautifully restored and refurbished to house this large restaurant and bar, it's a great use of a historic brick building. Featuring a menu that is approachable for business lunching, family dinners, or romantic meals, Dante's has entrees that range in style from Italian and Southwestern to seafood and great Montana steaks. Situated near the C.M. Russell Museum, it's often filled with a mix of local businesspeople and museum patrons.

Eddy's Supper Club, 3725 2nd Ave., Great Falls; (406) 453-1616; $$$. Opened in 1944 and still owned by the same family (three generations), this is one of Montana's most beloved supper clubs. The secret is the Campfire Steaks—made with a signature wine sauce and seared to perfection over an open flame. The trick works for the burgers, too. If you are man enough, try hoisting the twelve-ounce Campfire Burger off your plate. But don't forget the big martinis, slurped before supper in the comfortable embrace of the upholstered booths. Friday and Saturday nights you can get a real dose of lounge culture when the dueling piano players kick it up during dinner hours.

No time for dinner? Being a multipurpose Montana kind of place, Eddy's does double duty as a coffee shop and liquor store.

Empire Café, 214 West Main St., Lewistown; (406) 538-9912; $. This mainstay diner serves breakfast all day to ranchhands and retirees, but it's always bustling with the business of the day. In the early mornings, you'll hear the scrape of farmhand coffee mugs across the Formica counter, and later, when the 2 a.m. bar crowd gets out, you'll hear the silly late-night chatter and the sound of forks on plates as the revelers try to fend off the morning's hangovers.

5th Street Diner, 500 Central Ave., Great Falls; (406) 727-1962; $. Step back into the 1950s at 5th Street Diner, where the centerpiece is an original F. W. Woolworth lunch counter, all stainless steel and 65 feet long. It may be the last one in operation in the entire country; a similar section sits in the Smithsonian in Washington, D.C. The menu is 100 percent comfort food, from burgers and shakes to meat loaf.

The Freeze, 1722 Front St., Fort Benton; (406) 622-5071; $. The Freeze is an old-fashioned fast-food joint, circa 1950, located along the banks of the scenic Missouri River. It offers a full menu of burgers, hot dogs, various sandwiches, fries, chicken, shrimp, and fish. It's hard to beat one of the fourteen flavors of milkshakes on a hot summer day.

Ma's Loma Café, 203 U.S. Highway 87, Loma; (406) 739-4400; $. Most folks would pass through little Loma, a blink-and-you'll-miss-it town between Havre and Fort Benton, but for the fact that it is where the Marias River joins the Missouri. Lewis and Clark camped here on June 3, 1805, and they named the smaller river after Captain Lewis's cousin, Maria Wood. More to the point, however, is the Loma Café Nuevo (the "Nuevo" was tagged on recently by new Hispanic owners who bought this sportsman's staple in 2007). All the good stuff that the original "Ma" prepared is still on the menu: "The Sure Cure" for a hangover scramble with Polish sausage, eggs, toast, and hash browns; liver and onions; and an assortment of pies so varied, you'll want to order a piece of each. But new is the Thursday night Mexican menu, featuring three kinds of salsa, carne asada, tamales, enchiladas, and other authentic *comida*. It's good enough that you should time your trip to pass through here on a Thursday.

Mint Bar & Grill, 113 4th Ave. South, Lewistown; (406) 535-9925; $$$. Owners John Stelmack and John Adcock escaped from the exploding growth of Bozeman, a university town, for the respite of little Lewistown. It's a farming community smack in the middle of the state, and the two figured that the fishing and hunting were good, the sun always shines, and there wasn't much competition when it comes to gourmet food in town. That was back in 1998. Today, the corner restaurant is a favorite of locals and visitors alike. The menu is stacked with classics: steaks, of course, but what sets the cuisine apart is John Adcock's artful hand at making sauces with the richness of a French chef.

Nalivka's Original Pizza Kitchen, 1032 1st St., Havre; (406) 265-4050; $$. Everything is truly homemade at this take-out place tucked into the town's main thoroughfare. Nalivka's parents opened up the Original Pizza Kitchen in 1957, bringing the thick, doughy Chicago-style pizza to the state. Nalivka grew up in the kitchen and now bakes pies on her own with the help of her two sons. The pizza is truly unique, with a crust that is golden brown and flaky as a quiche and worth an order-in to your hotel. Ask for vegetarian options in sandwiches and pizzas, and they will gladly accommodate your needs—the VeeAnn's Gourmet with a béchamel sauce is a regular veggie option. Nalivka's offers traditional toppings, but also throws a little heritage into the mix, as in the German, which features country sausage and sauerkraut toppings.

Sip-N-Dip Tiki Lounge, 7th St. and 1st Ave. South, Great Falls; (800) 332-9819; www.ohairemotorinn.com; $. Rumors of mermaids have attracted even the most skeptical of people throughout the ages. In 2003 the guys at *GQ* ranked the Sip-N-Dip the number-one bar in the world, so I guess this marketing gimmick has been effective. The mermaids actually only come around on Friday and Saturday nights to cavort in the Ohaire Motor Inn pool, which has a window that opens to the bar. It's a fun place to order a cocktail and watch the show (if you are brave enough, you might take the plunge and swim with the mermaids yourself!). This is a local and tourist favorite that draws out the silliness in all of us; it's been around since 1962 and is still swimming.

Union Grille, Grand Union Hotel, 1 Grand Union Square, Fort Benton; (888) 838-1882 or (406) 622-1882; www.grandunionhotel .com; $$$. This exquisitely restored historic hotel is the flagship of tiny Fort Benton and the fare in the Union Grille and Bar is truly world-class gourmet. The culinary school–trained chef worked with Thomas Keller at the French Laundry in Napa Valley, California, and he applies every bit of the finesse he gleaned from that experience to his own menu.

While the menu changes seasonally and has a focus on fresh Montana ingredients whenever possible, it's details like the croutons on the house Caesar salad—hand-sliced, made to order, and served perfectly toasty, still warm on the greens. It's the fascinating cult wines on the eclectic list. It's the delicate homemade ice cream or petite molten chocolate cake. The food is continental cuisine, so you'll find Asian, European, and Cajun touches here and there, but only a deft hint, nothing overpowering.

It's also the ambience in the restaurant—white linen and silver, dramatic high ceilings in the 1884 building, elaborate detail around the tall windows. It's all just wonderful. Even in the morning, when a buffet breakfast is turned out with lavish convenience, the elegance remains. For a more casual experience, many people enjoy a meal in the bar or, during balmy summer months, on the patio by the river.

Walking the enchanting path along the town stretch of the mighty Missouri River is enough to make a road trip to this section of the state—this is where steamboat travel began and shipping furs and other goods created a commodity in Montana. Yet, notwithstanding the deep roots on the Lewis and Clark Trail and the fascinating history throughout the settling of the West, dining and staying at the Grand Union Hotel makes Fort Benton a destination on its own.

Brewpubs & Microbreweries

Belt Creek Brew Pub, 57 Castner St., Belt; (406) 277-3200. Belt Creek is not affiliated with the Harvest Moon Brewing Company, although it's just across town. In addition to Harvest Moon's Pig's Ass Porter, Belt Creek serves a wide range of microbrews on tap from Montana and beyond. No beer is brewed on site, despite the name, but it's a nice place to share some suds with friends.

Bert & Ernie's, 300 1st Ave. South, Great Falls; (406) 453-0601; www.bertandernies.com. Every local you meet will tell you that Bert

The Ubiquitous Mint Bar of Montana

It's by no means a franchise, yet it seems every town has one—from Froid to Sunburst. They range from swanky to downright stinky, but all are hard to resist once you begin your mission to have a drink in every one you pass. Most will surprise you if you give them a chance, and they're a great place to meet the locals.

One friend told me of his experience in White Sulphur Springs, getting ready for a fishing trip on the nearby Smith River. His group stopped into the Mint Bar, where the specialty of the house is "Nuclear Chicken" and there ain't no microbrews on tap, if you get the picture. Noticing long black scuff marks on the linoleum floor, he asked the barmaid about them. "We had a few bikers in last night," she replied. "They thought it would be fun to squeal wheels out of the bar." She shrugged. "Another day in the Mint."

In some places, as in Sunburst (where the Mint Bar doubles as a church), the establishments are more community gathering places than watering holes. In Great Falls during the early 1900s,

& Ernie's is the place to eat in Great Falls. Beer drinkers will tell you to try any one of the twenty brews they have on tap. I say, order the barbecue ribs. The casual menu is versatile and offers everything from gardenburgers to steaks, fit for all tastes.

Harvest Moon Brewing Company, 7 5th St., Belt; (406) 277-3188; www.harvestmoonbrew.com. Drawing on the abundance of Montana-grown barley and the pure, clean water of Belt, Harvest Moon set up its brewery in 1996. Though the town is tiny (700

the Mint Saloon was where cowboy artist C. M. Russell and his friends relaxed after work. The saloon provided the prolific artist the first public gallery for his works. (The Paris Gibson Square Museum of Art has the original back bar on display.) You never know who will be at the Mint Bar, but here are a few to stop by on your way through town.

Mint Bar & Café
88 Johannes Ave., Big Sandy
(406) 378-2679

Mint Bar
220 Main St., Shelby
(406) 434-3838

Mint Bar
237 Indiana St., Chinook
(406) 357-2730

Mint Bar
25 East 1st St. North, Sunburst
(406) 937-5555

Mint Bar
102 Main St., Froid
(406) 766-2333

Mint Bar
27 East Main St., White Sulphur Springs
(406) 547-9986

souls), being located only 17 miles from Great Falls allows the brewing company to service a lucrative market in a large urban center. Co-owner John Ballantyne has secured a handle on what was once a Pabst Blue Ribbon and Rainier market in Great Falls and has developed a loyal microbrew fan club. Pig's Ass Porter, Charlie Russell Red, and Coyote Ugly IPA are the three top sellers. You can find Harvest Moon brews at most local groceries in Montana. The taproom is open from 10 a.m. to 5 p.m., Monday through Friday.

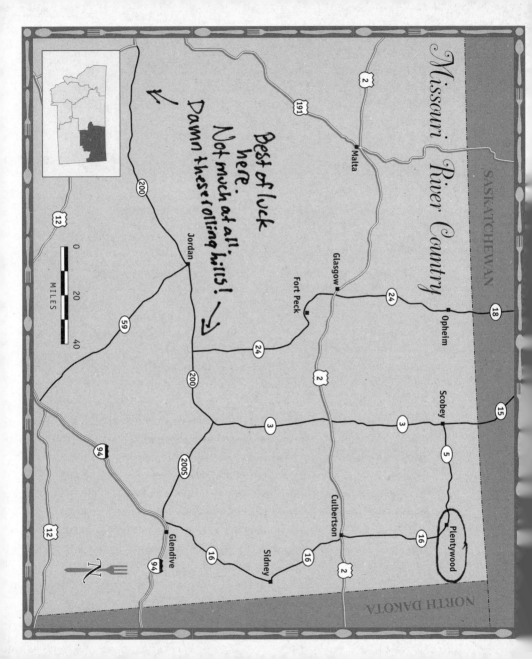

Missouri River Country (Northeast)

This part of the state has many names: The Big Open, The Big Dry, The Big Lonely. Out here, it's possible to drive 100 miles without seeing a farmhouse, town, or even another car on the road. When you do pass another traveler—car, truck, or tractor—it's customary to wave in acknowledgment. In my research for this stretch of the state, I drove 1,500 miles in five days, from Billings to Miles City, to the border of North Dakota, and far up north along the Hi-Line (the longest uninterrupted state highway in the United States), through such wide open spaces that there is no question why Montana is known as Big Sky Country. Wheat fields seem to unfurl endlessly to the horizon. Cattle graze on countless acres of grassy plains. Grain

THE HI-LINE

Don't drive it. Boring.

The western segment of U.S. Highway 2 extends from the Upper Peninsula of Michigan across the northern tier of the lower forty-eight states, bordering Canada. Most of the western route was built roughly paralleling the Great Northern Railway. U.S. 2 adopted the railway's route nickname, "The Highline," as the northernmost crossing in the United States. The most mileage on this route is within Montana, where it traverses the northern edge of the state from east to west, crossing some of the remotest country in Montana. The Hi-Line links dozens of desolate towns as it follows the Burlington Northern Santa Fe Railroad route, parallels the Missouri River, crosses four Native American reservations, touches the edge of Glacier National Park, and bridges the Continental Divide. It's also the remotest section of Montana, where the restaurants are few and far between.

elevators mark the clear landscape like monuments. Beauty takes a new form in such a sparse land, and a person gets hungry driving so many miles between one place and another.

That road trip also reminded me that restaurant options are few and far between given the remoteness of the country. When you do find a place to eat, there's not much on a typical menu that hasn't been frozen first and deep-fried before it hits your plate.

On the upside, however, there is pie. At any roadside diner, supper club, or cafe there are at least three different types of fresh-baked pie. Apple-blueberry. Lemon meringue. Peach-huckleberry. Pecan. Chess. Chokecherry. Strawberry-rhubarb. Coconut cream. The crusts are characteristically made from shortening or lard, but they are tried and true for perfect golden flakiness. You can always order it warm, and à la mode is customary. The best thing is that most eateries serve their pie presliced and on paper plates, anticipating that customers will ask for theirs to go since the portions in these parts are very generous. So my foolproof food lovers' tip for the northeastern part of the state is this: When in doubt, order the pie!

Made or Grown Here

Granrud's Lefse, 4886 Montana Highway 24 North, Opheim; (406) 762-3250; www.lefseshack.com. Twyla Anderson still makes the potato *lefse* recipe her grandmother taught her, using fresh ingredients and real potatoes. The Norwegian staple is available at groceries and specialty food shops throughout the state.

Little River Smokehouse, 445 Main St., Fort Belknap Agency, Harlem; (887) DRY-MEAT (379-6328) or (406) 353-2649; www.little riversmokehouse.com. Owned by the Gros Ventre and Assinaboine tribal communities, this business venture was just launching in 2009. Little River dries and smokes buffalo meat to produce excellently spiced jerky, summer sausage, meat sticks, and spicy sausage. USDA-inspected and approved, the smokehouse offers online sales.

Mahlstedt Ranch, Inc., 990 Rd. 422, Circle; (406) 485-2326; www.mahlstedtranch.com. Tender, flavorful, healthful beef that is born, raised, and fed on the Canen family cattle operation is essential in the "know where your food comes from" movement of today. Their Herefords are growth hormone–free and processed locally to your specifications. Ordering beef by phone is easy, or buy it at M3 Meats in Sidney or Ryan's Grocery & Processing in Jordan.

Specialty Stores & Markets

Bergie's, 410 Sargent St., Nashua; (406) 746-3441. A local treat in Nashua, this charming ice cream parlor on the edge of town scoops up really great-tasting homemade ice cream. Try an unusual seasonal flavor such as pink licorice, watermelon, or green apple. A "single" serving actually means two scoops, but what could be better than two scoops of smooth, creamy goodness on a hot day?

Farmers' Markets

Circle Farmers' Market, 311 Main St., Circle; (406) 485-2288. Saturday 8 a.m. to noon, July through September.

Glasgow Farmers' Market, Red Rock Plaza, Glasgow. Saturday 9 a.m. to 1 p.m., July through October.

Nashua Farmer's Market, 172 Balb Rd., Lions Park, by the Civic Center, Nashua; (406) 785-4731. Tuesday 5 p.m. to 6:30 p.m., July through September.

Sidney Farmers' Market, Richland Federal Credit Union, Sidney. Every second Friday 7:45 a.m. to noon, August through October.

Wolf Point Farmers' Market, 1436 Highway 528, Wolf Point; (406) 525-3330. Saturday 8 a.m. to 1 p.m., July through September.

Food Happenings

MARCH

Schmeckfest, Lustre; (406) 392-5735; www.lustrechristian.org. The little town of Lustre celebrates its homestead roots each year with "A German Festival of Tasting." The Lustre Christian High School fund-raiser is an all-you-can-eat German food buffet from 5 to 7 p.m. in mid-March. If you go, ask the folks of Lustre what *schmeck* means, as it seems there's some confusion. Some folks I asked said it means "delicious" and others said it translates to "a little taste." At any rate, the event draws hundreds of people from outlying communities who share in the German heritage that settled in these prairie hills.

JULY

Annual Governor's Cup Walleye Tournament and Community Fish Fry, Glasgow; (406) 228-2222. On Fort Peck Lake this is no small matter. The motto of walleye fishermen in Montana is this: Our fish are so big, you don't have to lie! Each year more than 200 teams of sportsmen bring in several hundred massive fish (the average catches are 10–12 pounds) and then fry 'em up! Nearly $40,000 in cash prizes are given away to participants in this community fund-raiser that helps the Fish, Wildlife, and Parks chapter control the walleye population in Fort Peck reservoir.

OCTOBER

Oktoberfest, Glasgow; (406) 228-2222. A fun family day in downtown Glasgow turns into a community harvest celebration, kicking off with a pancake breakfast and a children's parade. Later the pie- and hot dog–eating contest bring out the heavy competition. Look for good old-fashioned fun with outhouse races, tug of war, and a pumpkin-carving contest.

Beer-Battered Walleye (or Any Other Fish Fillets)

Recipe from Inge White, of Walleyes Forever.

12 ounces frozen fish fillets or 1½ pounds fresh fish fillets
2 eggs, separated
½ cup beer
¼ cup milk

1 cup flour
½ teaspoon seasoned salt (such as Lawry's or your own blend)
¼ teaspoon pepper

1. Preheat oven to 400°F. Generously butter heavy, large, cookie sheets.
2. Partially defrost fillets if frozen fish is used. Cut fish into pieces (3 inches by 1½ inches). Place on paper towels to dry.
3. Beat egg yolks until thick and light (reserve whites).
4. Blend in beer, milk, flour, and seasonings. Mix until smooth.
5. Beat egg whites until stiff but not dry and fold into batter. Pat fillets dry.
6. Dip fillets into batter, lift out, and drain slightly with fork or slotted spoon.
7. Fry in deep fat heated to 375°F for 2 to 3 minutes or until golden brown and puffed. Drain on paper towels. Serve with "chips" or salad.

Serves 4.

Sugar Beet Festival, Chinook; (406) 357-2017. Chinook is one of the largest sugar beet farm communities in the United States. They take their harvest celebration seriously in this town, so when Sugar Beet Festival rolls around after the crops have been harvested and shipped out, it's time to yell praise for agriculture. This community event rounds everybody up with a farmers' market, grain milling demonstrations, a bread-baking contest, a wheat diving coin toss for kids, and a cattle show, among many other activities.

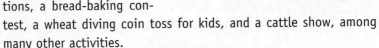

NOVEMBER

Wine and Food Festival, Sidney; (800) 331-7575. Once the sugar beet harvest is out the door, the town is full of smiles and ready to party a little. Sidney's Wine and Food Festival is held at St. Matthew's Parish Center and promises delicious food and samplings of Champagne, Chardonnay, or Zinfandel.

Landmark Eateries

Brown Bag Bistro, 172 South 1st Ave. East, Malta; (406) 654-1250; $$. Catering to the sportsman crowd that frequents Malta,

GIMME A DITCH

In Montana-speak, when folks walk into a saloon and order "a Ditch," that's shorthand for whiskey and water on ice.

a mother-daughter team serves breakfast and lunch. But they predominantly pack lunch to go for anglers on the Milk River or bird hunters in the field. Special orders are welcomed.

Fryar Tuck's and Robinhood Lounge, 520 West Railroad Ave., Plentywood; (406) 765-1153; $$. Any sportsman who has been to Plentywood has been to Fryar Tuck's and Robinhood Lounge and has fond memories. (Let's just clarify that the hearty souls in this town have a good sense of humor; there are no forests in Plenty*wood*.) The atmosphere is nothing special, but the steaks are good and the service is excellent. This could be one of the better meals in Montana if you go to Plentywood in just the right frame of mind.

Randy's Restaurant, 323 West 1st Ave., Plentywood; (406) 765-1661; $. The folks at Randy's Restaurant say it is in one of Montana's friendliest towns, and I'd have to agree. Randy and his wife, Bonnie, are in the kitchen cooking up the chicken-fried steak, burgers, and other meaty dishes.

Big Dry Country Powwows

Montana's seven reservations offer a wealth of cultural heritage and connection to Native American tribal history. Spring and summer bring bands of traditional celebrations through the state's communities. Most often the aroma of fry bread permeates the events, along with other foods that intermingle with the sound of drumming and galloping horses. For information on the annual Powwow calendar, go to www.visitmt.com/events.

Frequented by hunters who make Plentywood a tradition for fall forays, the town boasts folks who seem genuine to newcomers and the hospitality is as refreshing as the fresh pies baked daily at Randy's.

Shu's Kitchen, 506 1st Ave. East, Scobey; (406) 487-5347; $$. In regard to eating at this converted drive-in, a friend who lives in this charming Hi-Line town cautions, "Call ahead or Shu Mei will talk your ear off." Most folks in town eat here once a week and take their food to go, since Shu Mei is loquacious. The favorites: sweet and sour chicken and egg rolls. Owner and chef Shu Mei has been sautéing her Cantonese style of food in Scobey for twenty-seven years.

Slipper Lounge Restaurant, 608 Main St., Scobey; (406) 487-9973; $$$. When it's time to get dressed up for a date in Scobey, it's time to go to the Slipper. The historic building is this farming community's upscale restaurant, offering steak dinners, seafood, and other hearty entrees and a big slice of friendly small-town charm.

Bannock Bread or Indian Fry Bread

Recipe from Earl Old Person, Chief of the Blackfeet Nation; Montana Celebrity Cookbook *by Susie Beaulaurier Graetz.*

6 cups flour
3 tablespoons baking powder
1½ teaspoons salt
2½ cups water

1. Preheat oven to 350°F.
2. Stir together flour, baking powder, and salt. Gradually add water. (If dough is too dry, add more water.) Knead until dough is not sticky.
3. Grease a large baking pan, spread dough in pan, and bake 35 minutes.
4. Serve hot with chokecherry jelly and thin-sliced fried potatoes or beef from a roast, sliced thin and fried. Peppermint tea or coffee is usually served as well. This is a traditional meal for our people.

Stockman Bar & Steak House, 64 South 1st Ave. East, Malta; (406) 654-1919; $$. Malta is a hunter's paradise for the open country that creates incredible pheasant and other upland bird habitat. But when the sportsmen come in from the field, they go to the Stockman. Known for its barbecued baby back ribs and colorful company, it's a must in Malta.

Wild West Diner, 20 6th Ave., Culbertson; (406) 787-5374; $. The Wild West Diner has been a family-owned business for over twenty-seven years, offering great classic breakfast and lunches. Don't forget the fresh-baked pie to go.

Rolling Hills Winery, 220 6th St. West, Culbertson; (406) 787-5787. Rolling Hills Winery is in passionate pursuit of a wine culture in the eastern portion of the state. Winemaker George Nickoloff is in love with fruity wines and makes six different varieties from his homegrown raspberries and rhubarb. For the rest he buys fruit from local farmers to make chokecherry, honey, plum, and blueberry wines. George and his wife, Roxanne, welcome visitors to their production area and tasting room (attached to their car wash business) for an unforgettable sample.

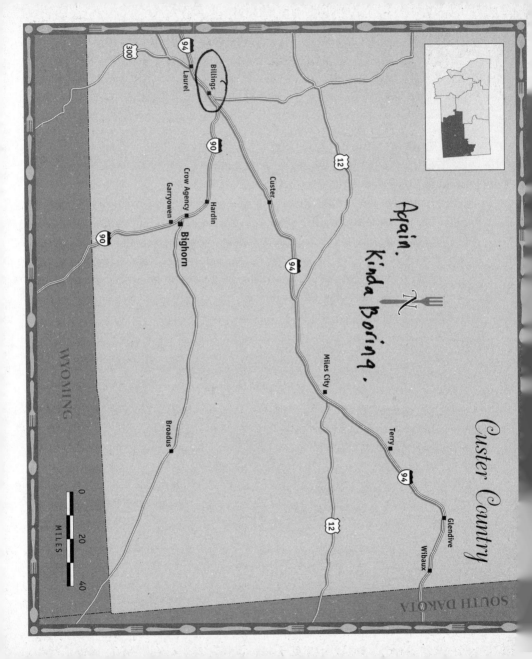

Custer Country (Southeast)

Home to Billings, Montana's largest metropolis, with a population around 100,000, Custer Country is at the edge of the state's vast open prairie. Here, the views stretch from the rimrocks of the Yellowstone River out to the easternmost stretches, where antelope outnumber the people two to one. This is Native American country and then hardscrabble homesteads, dryland farm country, and ranch land. The region's name refers to the Battle of the Little Bighorn, where General Armstrong Custer died and the U.S. Army suffered its greatest number of casualties in any territorial battle, though it still won the war that settled the West.

Except for in Billings proper, restaurants here are few and far between. The towns are sparse, the markets homespun, the people quiet but quick to smile. The pie can be divine. The hole-in-the-wall may serve the best meal you've ever tasted. Don't be afraid to log some miles and drive the back roads, open your senses to the wild landscape, and find a new out-of-the-way eatery.

Made or Grown Here

Danly Farms, 4112 Yard Office Rd., Laurel; (406) 628-6290. Mary Danly and Barbara Baresh have made an impact on the ultra-industrialized community of Billings by becoming the only certified organic farm in Yellowstone County. Just outside of Billings, Danly Farms sits on five acres of a former sixty-acre dairy farm that was subdivided several years ago; houses now "grow" where many former fields and pastures once yielded food. The old milking parlor has been converted to a greenhouse where tomato, pepper, and other plants were started from seed under fluorescent lights. They also produce spinach, arugula, and gourmet lettuce for Good Earth Market and the Billings Saturday farmers' market.

DDC Ranch, 294 South Park City Rd., Park City; (406) 633-2743; www.montanabison.org. Look for Craig and Julie Denney's ranch-raised bison at Good Earth Market in Billings. They promote their hormone-free healthy meat and swear by its natural flavor.

The Grapevine Ranch, P.O. Box 2363, Billings; (406) 690-4643; www.grapevineranch.com. Andrew and Jennifer Warren are proud to

DDC Ranch Bison Meatballs in Tomato Sauce

Meatballs

1 pound ground bison
2 tablespoons minced onion
1 teaspoon minced garlic
1 10-ounce package frozen
    spinach, thawed and
    drained
1 cup low-fat cottage cheese
1 egg
1 tablespoon water

Sauce

2 15-ounce cans tomato sauce
1 tablespoon garlic powder
1 tablespoon onion powder
1 tablespoon dried basil
2 tablespoons dried oregano

Meatballs

Mix ingredients together and form into balls approximately 1 tablespoon in size. In a pan, brown meatballs until firm.

Sauce

Combine all ingredients in a medium pot and heat thoroughly.

Pour sauce over meatballs. Simmer on the stove until all the flavors blend, 1 to 2 hours. Or place in a slow cooker and cook on low for about 4 hours.
Makes 24 meatballs, serves 4.

DDC Ranch
294 South Park City Rd., Park City
(406) 633-2743
www.montanabison.org

produce high quality grass-fed beef as a healthy, delicious alternative to the feedlot beef sold in most supermarkets today. All of their cattle are born and raised on the ranch, at the northern tip of the Big Horn Mountains, along the Bighorn River. The herd grazes on open pastures with native grasses and homegrown alfalfa and grass hay. You can order meat from the Web site or call directly. Packaged beef selections and custom orders can be arranged.

Martinson's Ranch Chocolates, 2359 North 8th Rd., Huntley; (888) 465-7386; www.ranchchocolates.com. Quite possibly the only chocolate ranchers anywhere, this Montana couple has switched from cattle to candy for their cash crop. Wynne and Joanne Martinson began selling their chocolates in 1985, and since then they've become a staple for holiday gift giving and year-round sweet treats. I first discovered their goodies when my daughter's soccer team began selling them as a fund-raiser. My favorite: Chocolate Nut Tumbleweeds, soft and smooth vanilla caramel, enrobed in rich milk chocolate then dredged in lightly salted buttery roasted almonds. Other folks rave about their Cream of Caramel bars. You can buy products online.

Montana Tamale Company, 520 Poplar Dr., Colstrip; (406) 748-3239; www.montanatamales.com. Using her grandmother's recipe, Reatha Montoya and her team of excellent tamale-makers hand make every tamale in the small production kitchen at Colstrip's Isabel Bills Community Center. They offer four tamale flavors: buffalo, beef, jalapeño chicken, and green corn. But it's the buffalo tamale that is the company specialty. Made from all-natural products without preservatives, these hearty, large tamales are available frozen from various grocery stores in the Billings area or can be shipped directly from Colstrip.

On Thyme Gourmet, 157 Hergenrider Rd., Bridger; (866) 998-4963; www.onthymegourmet .net. Wonderfully savory herbed butter (sage and basil, with or without garlic) and olive oil with basil or sage were this company's first products, in 2001. Since then Bonnie and Jack Martinell, who also own Boja Farm, have expanded their products to teas. The Montana basil is wonderfully energizing, and the sage has a delicate earthy flavor. On Thyme products are available online, at Good Earth Market in Billings, and at gourmet shops nationwide. All the herbs are grown on Boja Farm and are certified organic.

Rath Suffolks, P.O. Box 2215, Miles City; (406) 232-1060. This family-run sheep ranch is operated by Ray, Jane, and Cherie Rath. Their Suffolk lambs are available in health food markets and Town and Country grocery stores throughout Montana. The Suffolk originated in England from Southdown and Norfolk crosses; the breed was imported to the United States in 1888. The largest breed in the United States, it grows rapidly and the meat has a rich, gamy flavor.

Lamb Patties with Yogurt Mint Sauce

Recipe from the Montana Suffolk Sheep Breeders Association.

Lamb Patties

1 pound lean ground lamb
¼ cup dry bread crumbs
¼ cup chopped fresh mint
1 teaspoon lemon pepper

Yogurt Mint Sauce

⅔ cup plain yogurt
¼ cup firmly packed fresh mint
  leaves
1 teaspoon sugar

Lamb Patties

Gently mix together lamb, bread crumbs, mint, and lemon pepper. Shape into patties. Broil or grill 10 minutes or until desired doneness.

Yogurt Mint Sauce

Combine sauce ingredients in a blender or food processor and process until smooth with tiny flecks of mint. Serve sauce over patties.

Serves 4.

Seder Ridge Turkey Farm, 2476 South 27th Rd., Ballantine; (406) 967-2326. Pat Seder has been selling her farm-raised turkeys for nearly four decades. Along with her husband, Richard, she provides smoked turkeys and turkey eggs to Billings-area grocery stores. Good Earth Market in Billings always carries their products.

Prehistoric Delicacy

One of North America's largest freshwater fish, paddlefish (*Polyodon spathula*) are related to sturgeon. Scaleless and massive (adult paddlefish can weigh from 60 to 120 pounds; the state record paddlefish was 142 pounds, caught in 1973), they are classic examples of millions of years of ecological fine-tuning. The most striking feature of the paddler is its elongated paddle-shaped snout, which is used as an antenna for detecting food and helping the fish react to the river's changing current. They were introduced to the Yellowstone River in 1963. Most species of paddlefish are extinct, and as a result, the Fish, Wildlife, and Parks agency monitors the Montana populations near Glendive and Fort Peck closely. So far, the fish continues to be harvested as a sport fish, although with strict limits.

Because these river behemoths feed on microscopic organisms, live bait and lures are useless in catching them. Instead, fishermen use heavy-duty tackle to snag them. The season is short and centers around the town of Glendive, where more than 3,000 anglers flock to this short stretch of the Yellowstone River each year.

Excellent tasting, paddlefish have a versatile flavor and texture (and make a lot of fillets). A paddlefish can be frozen, canned, poached, steamed, smoked, baked, or sliced into steaks and grilled.

Royal Amandine Pan-Fried Paddlefish

Recipe from the Glendive Chamber of Commerce Paddlefish cookbook.

Paddlefish

1½ pounds paddlefish steaks or
   fillets, cut into pieces not
   more than 1 inch thick
¼ cup all-purpose flour
¼ cup cornmeal
½ teaspoon salt
½ cup (1 stick) butter

Sauce

½ cup (1 stick) butter
½ cup slivered almonds
1 tablespoon lemon juice
¼ teaspoon salt
 Dash of black pepper

1 tablespoon lemon juice
Parsley flakes for garnish

Paddlefish

1. Wipe fish pieces dry with paper towel. Roll pieces in a mixture of
   flour, cornmeal, and salt.

Trevino's Tortillas, 1102 Horn St., Billings; (406) 254-2336.
Billings native Chris Trevino uses his family recipe and fresh ingredients to make soft flour tortillas that are in great demand. Montana
grocery chains happily sell these homemade tortillas. Since they are
made without preservatives, they must be refrigerated; ask in a
nearby store to find out where they are stocked.

2. Melt butter in a shallow frying pan or electric skillet. Place fish pieces in the pan and cook slowly until brown on one side. Turn carefully and brown the other side. Cooking will take 10 to 15 minutes.
3. Remove pieces to a warm platter.

Sauce

1. Melt butter in a small saucepan. Add almonds and sauté over low heat to a delicate golden-brown color.
2. Add remaining ingredients and shake pan over heat for 2 minutes. (Variation: Toast the almonds before adding to melted butter. Do not sauté. Add remaining ingredients, blend, and heat carefully.)
3. Add lemon juice to the fish's hot butter drippings, blend thoroughly, and pour over paddlefish. Garnish with parsley flakes and serve at once with the sauce.

Serves 6–8.

Yellowstone Caviar, Glendive Chamber of Commerce & Agriculture, 808 North Merrill, Glendive; (406) 377-5601; www.glendivechamber .com/paddlefish/about_paddlefish.html. Here in the "Paddlefish Capital of the World," anglers flock to a stretch of the Yellowstone River that produces some of the rarest type of caviar. Since 1989, paddlefish roe has been harvested during the short spawning season (May 15 through June 30) and processed into caviar. A limit of

The Western Sustainability Exchange

The Western Sustainability Exchange (www.westernsustainability exchange.org) has organized a "Farm to Restaurant" program with eateries around the state. Connecting local agricultural producers to interested restaurants, the nonprofit group asks restaurateurs to sign and post a "Sustainability Pledge," stating that they serve locally grown or raised natural or organic foods. They agree to serve three meals per week that contain 50 percent local and sustainable ingredients and to train restaurant staff to promote the benefits of buying local and sustainable food.

1,000 fish are caught each year, which means the amount of roe collected fluctuates sometimes from 1,000 ounces up to 1,700 ounces. Regardless, the chamber sells out every year.

The small gray-black eggs have a mild flavor and are very similar in appearance to Russian Sevruga. Yellowstone Caviar sells for $20 an ounce. It's available directly from the Glendive Chamber or from most caviar-specific retailers (www.caviar.com). The chamber ships Yellowstone Caviar all over the world; the biggest customer is a caviar seller in Japan. Proceeds from the program are split between Fish, Wildlife, and Parks and the community of Glendive for recreational, historical, and cultural improvements.

Brockel's Chocolates, 117 North 29th St., Billings; (406) 248-2705. Gary Brockel just loves sweets. His shop is one of the first candy stores in Billings and remains a local favorite. You'll find all things dipped in chocolate at Brockel's—caramels, assorted delicious creams, nuts. But the best are the ice cream bars (made by Montana's own Wilcoxson's), hand dipped as you wait.

Candy Town USA, Inc., 820 Shiloh Crossing Blvd., Billings; (406) 651-9196; www.candytownusa.com. From old-fashioned favorites—Bottlecaps, Smarties Lollies, Red Hots—to Gross Out Alley—Box of Boogers and Gummy Maggots—this store is about sugary fun (although

Montana Sugar

Farms around Sidney, Montana, comprise one of the largest sugar beet–producing regions in North America (www.sidneysugars .com). Sugar beets are used to make 50 percent of the sugar consumed by the world (the rest comes from sugarcane). Look for American Sugar products in stores to find "Montana sugar."

there is a Sugar-Free Square for those with health concerns). The store expanded in 2008 and now features a cutely nostalgic soda fountain with antique counter and stools that serves up malts, shakes, sundaes, and the like. They serve Wilcoxson's Montana-made ice cream; I dare you to try the cinnamon-spice Firestick milkshake.

City Vineyard, 1640 Grand Ave., Billings; (406) 867-1491; www .cityvineyardwine.com. Sipping wine while shopping for your home cellar or that special dinner party is a wonderful amenity at this wine store. The large, organized display area is easy to navigate, and the shop holds regular wine and cheese pairings and always serves up the monthly offerings by the glass. It's a mutually beneficial selling tool that allows you to absorb all the adjectives that describe the latest and greatest vintages, as well as the subtleties of artisanal cheeses.

The Coffee Den, 104 South Merrill Ave., Glendive; (406) 377-4938. Glendive's first espresso rode into town in 2001, right next to the Book n' Bear Nook in the historic Dion Building. While waiting for your latte, browse their home decor and furnishings from local artists, books by local authors, and Montana-made products. You may happen in on a weekend when Sunday brunch is on the docket (occasional), but otherwise there are always made-from-scratch goodies to choose from. On any given day that includes pies, quiche, cheesecakes, sandwiches, salads, soup, and breads.

The Copper Colander, 2440 Grant Rd., Billings; (406) 294-9628; www.coppercolander.com. For a true foodie, a visit to this massive gourmet store is as satisfying a way to spend an afternoon as a trip to a museum would be for an artist. It's cooking gadgets galore here (thousands of them!), on top of the fact that there's a showcase kitchen, shelves of specialty food and coffee items that lean heavily on Montana-made products, and just the atmosphere of other people who are *really* into food. Owner Sharon Culbertson and her staff offer weekly cooking classes on everything from canning to cutlery, as well as the Create a Chef series of courses for kindergarteners through high schoolers.

Good Earth Market, 3024 2nd Ave. North, Billings; (406) 259-2622; www.goodearthmontana.com. Providing local, organic, and fresh produce, along with other delicious products, this nonprofit cooperative grocery store is as much a community resource as it is a place to buy food. Part of the mission statement is to support local growers and producers, and about 22 percent of the products here come from local suppliers. There is an excellent bulk food section and a healthy deli. Wine and artisanal cheese is offered, too.

Grains of Montana, 926 Grand Ave., Billings; (406) 259-7142; www.grainsofmontana.com. This artisan bakery was founded by Nielsen Farms, which has grown and harvested wheat in nearby Nashua since 1965. Every loaf of bread from this bakery and restaurant is all-natural, without fillers or stabilizers. The Nielsens refer to the "bread cycle" with reverence. They grow McNeal wheat on 15,000 acres and know every step of the harvest, milling, refining, and baking process personally. Each loaf is made from scratch the

Grains of Montana
Peanut Butter Blossoms

1¾ cups Grains of Montana All-
  Natural white flour
½ teaspoon salt
1 teaspoon baking soda
½ cup (1 stick) butter
½ cup peanut butter

½ cup sugar
½ cup brown sugar
1 egg
1 teaspoon vanilla
2 tablespoons milk
Chocolate kisses

1. Preheat the oven to 375°F.
2. Sift together the flour, salt, and baking soda.
3. Cream the butter and peanut butter.
4. Gradually add both sugars. Add unbeaten egg, vanilla, and milk. Add the dry ingredients.
5. Shape dough into balls, roll in sugar, and bake for 8 minutes.
6. Remove from the oven and top with chocolate kisses, pushing down on cookies. Bake 2–3 minutes longer.

Makes 2 dozen cookies.

Grains of Montana
926 Grand Ave., Billings
(406) 259-7142
www.grainsofmontana.com

old-fashioned way, allowing the dough the time it needs to ferment properly (at least twelve hours) and to rise naturally. This lends the bread its hearty, savory texture.

Grains of Montana started with just one bakery and restaurant (serving hearty breakfasts and lunch sandwiches) in 2004. It's grown in leaps since then, establishing a franchise and building a commercial bakery operation (there are locations in Biloxi, Mississippi; Meridian, Idaho; and Tucson, Arizona). Soon your local grocery store may be stocking Grains of Montana breads.

Kafe Utza, 19 South 9th St., Miles City; (406) 234-9821; www.kafeutza.com. A splash of trendy, urban coffee shop swank with a Wi-Fi hot spot never hurts a little rural town. Kafe Utza brews and roasts coffee and specializes in fine pastries to go with it. Owner Kara Stewart decided to embrace her Basque heritage while naming her coffee shop; *kafe utza* is the Basque term for "black coffee."

Made in Montana Gifts, 315 North Merrill, Glendive; (406) 377-4797. A new initiative to launch a "Buy Local" campaign and organize a "Farm to Market" program, promoting farmers and ranchers in the area, has boosted the shelves of this Made in Montana shop. Locally produced products include Western Trails Food pancake mixes, Montana Grassland Mixes pancake and bread mixes, Whoop Up Creek loofahs and soaps, and many other gift items.

Miles City Books & News, 907 Main St., Miles City; (406) 234-8136. With the wide selection of titles comes a cup of hot coffee and great service. The store stays open late for the bookish coffee klatch–types.

Paula's Edibles, 2712 Second Ave. North, Billings; (406) 655-0865; www.paulasedibles.com. Along with the coffee drinks, Paula's serves up cute and creative locally made chocolates that have a Montana twist. The Bear Claw (shaped like a grizzly footprint) is my favorite and makes for a fun gift item. Owners Larry and Sarah Ferro (Paula was the original owner) make all the chocolates at the shop, including specialty chocolate-dipped cookies, pretzels, and cinnamon bears.

Poet Street Market, 905 Poly Dr., Billings; (406) 245-9501; www.poetstreet.com. The daily selection at Poet Street Market is overwhelming—salads, soups, and the pizza du jour and sandwiches to order. Plus the desserts, which are typically so delectable-looking that choosing one could take a good fifteen minutes of deliberation time (Italian cream cake, three-tiered mini cake, truffles, cheese-cakes, sour cream–pear tart, and special orders).

Like a true deli, Poet Street offers a half dozen or more salads, from broccoli to pasta concoctions to creamy cucumber. The breads are baked daily—French baguettes, ciabatta, and other European-style breads—and hand-sliced thick for sandwiches. The seasonal

Pumpkin Harvest sandwich—house-baked pumpkin bread, sliced turkey, and cranberry-apple compote—is good enough to crave all year long. The market also carries a line of specialty food products and cookbooks.

Rock Creek Coffee Roasters, 124 North Broadway, Billings; (406) 896-1600; www.rockcreekcoffee.com. Joel and Peggy Gargaro fell in love with Billings in 2004 and found a niche with a little downtown coffee shop. They roast their own blends, and the wonderful smell wafts through the store, where businesspeople and students take advantage of the free Wi-Fi and friendly atmosphere.

Simply Wine, 517 South 24th St. West, Billings; (406) 651-5985; www.simplywinestore.com. Casually called "the wall of wine," this shop features a remarkable collection of wines that scored 90 points or better according to *Wine Spectator* and *Wine Enthusiast* magazines yet are priced under $20. Unheard of? Not here, where the owners try to pair fair prices with fine wines. Value isn't the only highlight at this wine shop; interesting varietals and vintages are available and a monthly wine club provides great exposure to the world of wine.

Sod House Sundries, 1506 Crisafulli Dr., Glendive; (406) 377-1842; www.sodhousesundries.com. Far from the sweet heat of Mexico, Texas, Colorado, Arizona, California, and New Mexico, but no less passionate about the spice of life, this specialty food store is dedicated to hot sauces. Dedicated salsa lovers, Cary and Steve have traveled to hither and yon to find the best dipping sauces, marinades, salsas, barbecue rubs and sauces, and (for a sweet balance) honey butters. This small shop is filled with jars of their favorite brands. Shipping is available.

Farmers' Markets

Annual Roundup Saturday Market, Busy Bee Cafe on 317 1st Ave. West, Roundup. Saturday 9 a.m. to 1 p.m., May through September.

Columbus Farmers' Market, Railroad Park on Pike Ave., Columbus. Thursday 4 to 6:30 p.m., July through September.

Downtown Laurel Farmers' Market, Town Square Park, 1st Ave., Laurel. Wednesday 4 p.m. until dark, July through September.

Hardin Farmers' Market, Little Horn State Bank parking lot, Hardin. Friday 7:30 a.m. to noon, August through mid-September.

Miles City Farmers Market, Riverside Park, Miles City. Saturday 8 a.m. to noon (except during the Bucking Horse Sale weekend), May through October; Tuesday 6 p.m. to 8 p.m. beginning mid-July.

Yellowstone Valley Farmers' Market, Broadway St., at the Skypoint structure, downtown Billings. Saturday 8:30 a.m. to noon, July through October.

Farm Stands

Alfred's Garden, East Glendive; (406) 939-0731. Farmer Alfred Cron sells his fresh produce from June to October at the Glendive farmers' market each week. He brings a variety of garden lettuce, spinach, peas, carrots, beans, beets, cucumbers, potatoes, bell and hot peppers, kohlrabi, cabbage, melons, squash, and tomatoes. When the abundance of the season overwhelms, he places an ad in the local weekly paper for the you-pick season. Times and days vary; call for more details.

Boja Farm, 157 Hergenrider Rd., Bridger; (406) 664-3010; www .onthymegourmet.net. Just an hour from Billings, Boja Farm grows a variety of country-hearty fruit, herbs, and garlic. Farmers Bonnie and Jack Martinell are committed to sustainable farming; all their products are certified organic. They sell produce at local farmers' markets, Good Earth Market in Billings, and straight from the farm (call for directions). Boja also produces On Thyme Gourmet herbs, seasonings, and teas. At the farm you can pick your own raspberries (red, yellow, and purple) in August and apples come September. Open 8 a.m. to 7 p.m. from June through mid-October.

Bluewater Orchard, 1088 Bridger-Fromberg Backroad, Fromberg; (406) 995-4773 or (480) 223-8934. Early season apples begin ripening in the middle of August, and if the gate is open at Bluewater Orchard, come on in to pick up some. With about a hundred trees, the orchard grows Duchess, Yellow Transparent, and Crimson Beauty, which are good for making applesauce, baking, and sausage-making. Grown pesticide and herbicide free, they usually sell for around $1 per pound. If you can't make it to the orchard, Bluewater also offers delivery anywhere near Bozeman, Billings, Butte, Ennis, or Big Sky. Open July to October.

Food Happenings

MAY

Micro Brew Festival, Billings. The annual Billings Micro Brew Festival is a massive event (usually 5,000 people attend) featuring more than sixty kegged microbrews, ciders, and root beers, along with the addition of over forty imported beers and "malternatives," gourmet foods, and forty bottled wines. It is held at the Shrine Auditorium, 1125 Broadwater Ave.

Pie in the Park, Miles City. Eastern Montana Fairgrounds, 42 Gary Owen Rd. (406) 234-2890; www.buckinghorsesale.com. An extension of the festivities that surround the world-famous Miles City Bucking Horse Sale (the social event of the year), Pie in the Park has become a tradition that's taken very seriously among bakers. Each year, around forty pies are entered in this judged contest. First prize is $100, but the real reward is to have blue-ribbon bragging rights for a year. Entries in the homey culinary event range from classics like pecan, berry medley, and apple to more unusual combinations such as pineapple, bread pudding, buttermilk pie, strawberry-mango, and caramel apple. A panel of six judges grades the pies on a 600-point scale and takes their pie very seriously.

Wine and Food Festival, Billings. (406) 657-2244; www.wine foodfestival.com. A benefit for Montana State University–Billings, this weeklong fund-raiser brings top winemakers and chefs to town for a host of elaborate dinners and wine seminars each year. The event kicks off with an "Iron Chef" competition, pitting local chefs against one another for a live cook-off while hungry guests wait, watch, and judge the savoriest dishes. Seated with the guests, a panel of judges from other regional restaurants cast their votes to determine Billings's King Chef. Tickets are limited, but open to the public.

AUGUST

Mexican Fiesta, Billings. South Park. (406) 208-0103. The bright colors of Mexico hit the streets in a parade that ends at South Park in Billings, where one day a year the aroma of homemade tortillas wafts through the air. With the goal of sharing Mexican culture with the community, the

Fiesta has been an annual event for more than half a century. Close to 5,000 people gather around booths selling food and fun, leading to a traditional Mexican dinner, dancing, and a silent auction to benefit a local church.

SEPTEMBER

Ales for Trails, Billings. (406) 247-8637; www.bikenet.org/events. Your taste buds will go crazy with the selection of brews from across the region, great food, and music to raise funds for an urban bike (and pedestrian) trail network. More than forty different microbrews from Billings and beyond are offered for this annual fund-raiser that helps create a bicycle-friendly community. Since the event began in 2001, more than $100,000 has been raised to develop a working trail system. The party is from 4 to 10 p.m. at Billings Depot (downtown on Montana Avenue).

OCTOBER

HarvestFest, Billings. Sky Point, 2815 2nd Ave. North. (406) 294-5060; www.harvestfun.com. Celebrating the change of seasons, this finale event downtown brings food vendors, arts and crafts, and farmers' market vendors together for one last hurrah before winter.

Bin 119, 119 North Broadway, Billings; (406) 294-9119; $$$. For wine lovers, this is an unexpected surprise with a stylish casual atmosphere and an outstanding selection of wines—180 labels and around 30 wines sold by the glass. The menu is inspired by Spanish tapas, or small-plate cuisine, perfect for light dinners or for sharing many flavors with friends.

Café Italia, 2417 Montana Ave., Billings; (406) 869-9700; www .cafeitaliabillings.com; $$. Opened in 2008, Café Italia is locally owned by chef Steve Marsh, who helped renovate a 1910 brick building in the downtown historic district. The traditional Italian dishes are many, but probably the best aspect of the menu are the sketches of different pasta shapes: orecchiette, bucatini, fusilli, pappardelle—explained at last!

Cattle-ac, 420 Pacific Ave., Miles City; (406) 234-6987; $$$. Across from the defunct, but historic railroad depot, this steak house anchors the community with consistently good food. A wide array of comfort food is served—prime rib is the favorite, but all the Angus steaks are first rate. Order the fries; they are excellent.

The Dizzy Diner, 316 East Spring St., Terry; (406) 635-4666; $. Halfway between Miles City and Glendive, this cute 50s-style diner (it was once a drive-in) is the perfect place to stop for a break from the road. Clean, bright, red and white, it's a sweet respite before heading into the badlands up near Glendive, where most people go to explore Makoshika State Park. The menu consists of wraps, salads, and breakfast dishes (served all day), all offered up on brightly colored Fiestaware. Milkshakes, sundaes, and several flavors of freshly baked pie are the daily treats.

The Granary Restaurant, 1500 Poly Dr., Billings; (406) 259-3488; www.billings-granary.com; $$$$. Built in 1935, the Granary served as the milling department for Billings Polytechnic Institute until World War II. The building was not used again until the Granary Restaurant opened in 1976. It was remodeled in 2004 under new ownership and reinvented as a contemporary eatery in a historic building. The classics—steak and seafood—are interpreted here with a finesse that results in an unforgettable meal. A cocktail list and New World wine list speak of the intentions here, appealing to a very food- and beverage-savvy clientele.

The restaurant serves naturally aged hand-cut beef from Misty Isle Farms in Washington. The beef is cooked perfectly to your taste in a high-temperature broiler. Maybe it's the fact that it is naturally raised and pasture-fed free from antibiotics, hormones, or growth stimulants or maybe it's the way it's cooked, but it will be arguably one of the best steaks you'll ever eat.

Juliano's, 2912 7th Ave. North, Billings; (406) 248-6400; $$$. It's hard to categorize chef and owner Carl Kurokawa's cuisine. The Hawaiian-born chef combines Asian and European influences in the contemporary fusion style. The result is always unique and sometimes adventurous; think roasted ostrich, grilled elk, spicy watermelon salad. Set in a historic 1902 Victorian home and converted into a restaurant, the locals are regularly drawn to this out-of-the-way spot. Quiet, quirky, and quintessentially gourmet is how I'd describe Juliano's. The fish is flown in fresh, the menu changes monthly, and special wine dinners are featured throughout the year.

McCormick Café, 2419 Montana Ave., Billings; (406) 255-9555; www.mccormickcafe.com; $. Along with the claim to the "best omelets in Billings," McCormick also serves crepes "from the streets of Paris." Maybe not quite Paris, but pretty darn good, served up with traditional sugar and a wedge of lemon, a combination of mixed fruit toppings, or the popular (and this writer's favorite) European Nutella spread.

If French is not your thing, try the Toucan Breakfast, scrambled eggs with onions and mushrooms baked with layers of bacon, tomato, and Swiss cheese on white bread and spread with scallion cream cheese; it's hearty and savory. The espresso is also very good.

Set in the heart of the business district and close to local hotels, this is a breakfast and lunch joint for both locals and tourists. The historic quality, with exposed brick, pressed tin ceilings, and schoolhouse lighting makes for a comfortable atmosphere.

The Montana Bar, 612 Main St., Miles City; (406) 234-5809; $. Without hesitation, I can say that this is the best saloon in Montana. From the street, the neon sign shaped like the state only hints at how cool this place is. Anyone in Miles City will admit it has been an icon since the founding of this cowtown. Montana Bar doesn't serve food, but inside the dark mahogany wood of the ornate 1850s Brunswick bar beckons. Look around at the classic leather booths, the black-and-white marble tile floor, the smoky smell that is somehow sultry rather than offensive. Since 1902, the Montana has been a gathering place. The steer hanging on the walls could tell stories of Gene Autry buying a round of drinks in the 1950s, not to mention the land and cattle deals struck over a drink between local Range Riders.

Purple Cow, 1003 Route 1, Hardin; (406) 665-3601; $. This is basically a truck stop, but it's a friendly joint where I go when I'm *really* hungry. Serving up great home-style meals since 1971, Purple Cow bakes all the breads and rolls daily and serves a selection of freshly baked pies. A regular's favorite, the Montana Breakfast, was featured in *Reader's Digest*—it's a half pound of bacon, sausage, or ham, four large eggs, twelve pancakes, three-quarters of a pound of hash browns, and a pint of orange juice. The famous BIG BLT is served on a home-made whole wheat hoagie bun with nine strips of bacon, six slices of tomato, and loads of lettuce. I like to stick with the pie. The roadside restaurant is located north of Hardin on Montana Highway 47.

Q Restaurant, 2503 Montana Ave., Billings; (406) 245-2503; www.qcuisine.com; $$$. This swanky urban-styled restaurant and cocktail lounge has infused a new level of sophistication into the Billings food scene. With a menu that is one part Asian, one part Italian, and two parts American amalgam of comfort food (read: steak, seafood, pasta), innovative chef Daniel Roberts presents even the classics with a sophisticated twist. Take the tenderloin and foie gras entree: by serving the foie next to a classically cut grilled steak, Roberts opens up customer palates to a rich culinary journey. Other relatively daring items appear on the appetizer menu in particular—the ahi tower, pan-roasted quail, sweet potato gnocchi, edamame.

Set in the historic Carlin Hotel, Q is part of a wonderful renaissance in downtown Billings. The atmosphere in the main restaurant and lounge elegantly blend early-twentieth-century features (vaulted, pressed tin ceilings) with Modern style.

The Rex, 2401 Montana Ave., Billings; (406) 245-7477; www.therexbillings.com; $$$. Built in 1910 as the Rex Hotel, this is a true Billings landmark. It was once the anchor of this big city, with "celebrities" visiting as regulars up through the 1920s, including Buffalo Bill Cody, Calamity Jane, and Will James. Back then, original chef Alfred Heimer (Buffalo Bill's cook for the Wild West Show) settled in Billings and advertised the hotel's "Buffalo Bill Bar" as a premier meeting place, where they guaranteed "cold beer and good German lunches."

The Rex remains the community's favorite gathering place and is best known for its tried and true steaks (certified Angus beef). The Garlic Roasted Filet is a classic and the Montana Avenue New York

Steak, topped with two jumbo shrimp and shiitake mushroom sauce, is a perennial favorite. Add fine, consistent food to the enthralling historic atmosphere, and it's a dining experience fit for a king, as the name implies (in Latin).

Rocket Gourmet Wraps & Sodas, 2809 1st Ave. North, Billings; (406) 248-5231; www.rocketwraps.com; $. In America's love of wrapping crazy ingredients into a tortilla, Rocket Wraps hasn't forgotten where that fast food phase began: the basic burrito. They still offer the Plain Jane—ground beef, red beans, cheddar cheese, sour cream, romaine lettuce, and housemade tomato salsa—for those of us who become confused by all the *other* options these days. But for the adventuresome, this wrap place has its own twists, from Thai to bayou, Alfredo to curry. The menu is like a fast trip around the world, say, in a rocket.

600 Café, 600 Main St., Miles City; (406) 234-3860; $. The scrape of coffee cups across the well-worn Formica countertop early in the morning at this authentic cowboy diner is the first clue that this is a good ol' boys hangout. A row of low swiveling stools faces the glass cooler of homemade pies and the sign overhead that reads: WELCOME TO THE SIMPLE LIFE. The dress code is ideally a cowboy hat and boots, a plaid shirt if you are really in the swing, but this is a come-as-you-are kind of place. Large-format hand-tinted photos of rodeo and ranching scenes circa 1950 line the wall above the booths and the deco-style tile floor is as iconic as the clientele. On the menu is the typical breakfast fare, but diners with this small-town atmosphere are hard to find these days and that's what makes the 600 worth visiting. Order the biscuits and gravy or chicken-fried steak if you are especially hungry, but for me it's all about the pie.

Stella's Kitchen and Bakery, 2525 1st Ave. North, Billings; (406) 248-3060; $. The perfect breakfast spot, Stella's is just off the downtown historic business center. It's the place for the basic omelet or eggs to order with homemade bread as toast. But the real draw is Stella's ooey-gooey sixteen-ounce caramel rolls—doughy, buttery, sugary! Is it breakfast or dessert? You decide.

Stoneville Saloon, U.S. Highway 212, P.O. Box 97, Alzada; (406) 828-4404; $. Who knew that at the center of the nation was a saloon? Yet when driving this long and barren stretch of America, the Stoneville Saloon pops up on U.S. Highway 212 like an oasis. The middle of nowhere, you may say, but actually it's on the way to a lot of places. It is 163 miles east of the Little Bighorn Battlefield. Forty miles north of Devil's Tower National Monument, on the edge of the Northern Black Hills, 36 miles west of Belle Fourche, South Dakota, and 80 miles south of Medicine Rocks Park. And with all that driving, a classic Whiskey Ditch (Jim Beam and water on ice) sounds like a decent idea. Like the honest landscape you'll see endlessly framed by the windshield, the folks at Stoneville don't hide anything. A sign on the front of the building clearly reads: CHEAP DRINKS; LOUSY FOOD. That depends on your perspective, but I'd recommend the Nitro Chili as a fine bowl of edible goodness.

Sweet Ginger, 2515 Montana Ave., Billings; (406) 245-9888; $$. These days, that old adage about not eating seafood if you are a hundred miles from an ocean is a mistake. With overnight shipping companies servicing any urban area in the country, it's become more common to fly in fresh fish several times a week. Ask the folks at Sweet Ginger, where they make gorgeously fresh sushi rolls every day—spicy tuna rolls, unagi, California rolls. It's all here at this upscale Asian bistro. Chinese food items are offered also, but I stick with the sushi. Montana may be the country, but it's not uncivilized.

Walkers Grill, 2700 1st Ave. North, Billings; (406) 245-9291; www .walkersgrill.com; $$$. In 1993, owner Bill Honaker opened this res- taurant in another location and quickly received accolades for a menu that coupled approachable flavors with sophisticated cuisine under the moniker of American style. When he moved in 2005 and redesigned the restaurant's concept, keeping the American but adding tapas (small plates) for the swanky Western-inspired bar, the loyal local clientele followed. Walker's started a trend of urban minimalism in Billings, when it comes to the ultramodern yet somehow Western decor.

The food, however, only got better. Housemade pasta is featured daily, along with impressive original renditions of classic seafood (halibut, salmon, prawns) and the ubiquitous Montana steaks (ten- derloin and New York cuts). But the high point of the culinary offer- ings is the buffalo osso bucco. The twenty-two ounces of Star Ranch

100 percent natural smoked buffalo (enough to share with several fellow diners) is slow-braised for six hours in Cabernet Sauvignon and served in its own juices over mashed potatoes.

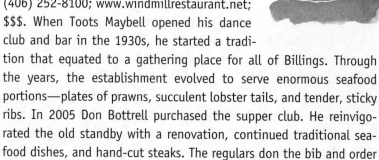

 The Windmill Supper Club, 3429 TransTech Way, Billings; (406) 252-8100; www.windmillrestaurant.net; $$$. When Toots Maybell opened his dance club and bar in the 1930s, he started a tradition that equated to a gathering place for all of Billings. Through the years, the establishment evolved to serve enormous seafood portions—plates of prawns, succulent lobster tails, and tender, sticky ribs. In 2005 Don Bottrell purchased the supper club. He reinvigorated the old standby with a renovation, continued traditional seafood dishes, and hand-cut steaks. The regulars don the bib and order up a heaping plate of king crab legs. Butter, anyone?

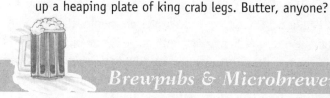

Brewpubs & Microbreweries

Angry Hanks Brewing, 2405 First Ave. North, Billings; (406) 252-3370. Owner and brewer Tim Mohr doesn't promote his beers or advertise his brewpub; he doesn't even have a Web site. So far he doesn't need to, as the "neighbors" line up when it's beer-thirty (actually around 4 p.m., when the taproom opens) for what's on tap. Most of his beer is sold straight from the brewery, and this is where "Hoppy Hour" begins for microbrew fans in downtown Billings.

Named for a perpetually grumpy friend, the tongue-in-cheek anger continues as a theme in the beer names: Anger Management Belgian Wheat, Head Trauma IPA, and so on. The brewery is an old gas station that's been converted to an industrial-cool space that's easy to spend time in with a few pints and good friends.

Beavercreek Brewery, 104 Orgain Ave., Wibaux; (406) 795-BEER (2337). With just over 500 souls in Wibaux, the guys at Beavercreek Brewery are in the business for the love of it. The town is nearly on the Montana–North Dakota border; I guess you could say that Wibaux is *only* three and a half hours from Billings or *on the way* to Bismarck (162 miles) or eventually Fargo (361 miles). It takes a lot of pluck to start a microbrewery far from the urban crowds that might be open to new flavors. Beavercreek produces four basic beers (all unfiltered)—Wibaux's Gold, Beaver Creek Pale Ale, Redheaded IPA, and Paddlefish Stout (served with a chocolate chip cookie). Owners Jim Devine and Sandy Stinnett moved from home brewers to master brewers when they opened in 2008 with a stuffed beaver as a mascot and the tagline "Our beavers taste better than your beavers." So far off the beaten path, yet so good.

Carter's Brewing, 2526 Montana Ave., Billings; (406) 252-0663; www.cartersbrewing.com. Named for brewer and owner Michael Uhrich's son, this craft beer maker won the 2009 Brewer's Association Award. Not bad for a guy who got his start in the brewing world by making beer at home. He progressed to the commercial scene with a job as a brewer at Yellowstone Brewing Company from 2001 to 2007, before opening his own place nearby. Prone to experimentation, Uhrich has followed his passion and readily changes the lineup in the historic building down by the tracks. The railroad theme serves him well, with catchy names for brews, such as Trainwreck Imperial IPA, Switchyard Scottish Ale, and three "signature beers": Handcar Hefe, Derailed IPA, and Black Magic Porter. My favorite is La Grisette Farmhouse Ale (spiced with chamomile); it's a lighter version of a French-style Saison and the perfect summer heat chaser.

Montana Brewing Company, 113 North Broadway, Billings; (406) 252-9200; www.montanabrewingco.net. Montana Brewing Company is clean and straightforward when it comes to a brewpub, keeping the brews and the atmosphere simple in order to have broad appeal. Located in Billings's historic downtown, Montana Brewing won "Best Small Brewpub and Small Brewpub Brewer" at the 2007 Great American Beer Festival. It dishes out wood-fired pizzas and buffalo burgers during lunch (11 a.m. to 2 p.m.) to go with the lineup of flagship beers: Whitetail Wheat, Fat Belly Amber, Sandbagger Gold, Sharptail Pale Ale. All are named with a nod to the culture of wild game hunting in the High Plains. My favorite is the medium-bodied flavor of the Fat Belly Amber. (Referring to the state of a prime doe, rather than to the status of my own middle after drinking a couple of these, I presume.) The substantial list of seasonal brews keeps the lineup here interesting and fresh. I'd head back here in the fall for a pint of Custer's Last Stout for sure.

Pub Crawl

Four brewpubs make up an unofficial Brewery District in downtown Billings—Angry Hanks, Carter's, Montana Brewing Company, and Yellowstone Valley Brewing. They're all within four blocks of one another, making it easy to walk (or crawl) amiably from one pub to the next on your own tasting tour.

Yellowstone Valley Brewing, 2123-B First Ave. North, Billings; (406) 245-0918; www.yellowstonevalleybrew.com. The goodtime brew crew is made up of chief brewer and owner George Moncure, brewers Caleb Lausch and Ryan Koga, and taproom manager Donnie Veltri. Together they make business fun, operating a music venue in the Garage Pub and crafting solid brews on tap and in bottles, available from the taproom or in local stores throughout the state (and as far as Oklahoma!). Saturdays bring music to the pub, from bluegrass to rock.

Worth a try is the Renegade Red ESB (sweet with a malty extra-special bitter flavor to follow and the ruby red color hopped to balance the malty-sweet style). But Moncure counts the Wild Fly Ale, an elegant and mellow-tasting amber, as his signature brew.

Appendix A: Food Happenings

Appendix B: Specialty Foods

The following shops and businesses are especially known for these items that they produce or grow.

Asian Food
Asia West Mart (Deer Lodge), 81–83, 85

Breads and Bakery Goods
Bagelworks (Bozeman), 17–18
Baker Bob's Big Stack Bakery (Great Falls), 188
Bear Paw Coffee Shop & Deli (Big Sandy), 188
Booze & Buns (Sheridan), 85
Elle's Belles Bakery and Café (Bozeman), 20–21
Grains of Montana (Billings), 235–37

Great Northern Foods (Bigfork), 129–30
Hempl's Bakery (Great Falls), 190
Joe's Pasty Shop (Butte), 84
Nancy McLaughlin's Pasty Shop (Butte), 84
Park Avenue Bakery & Café (Helena), 88–89
Park Street Pasties (Butte), 84
On the Rise (Bozeman), 27–28
Sweetgrass Bakery (Helena), 89–90
Town Talk Bakery (Butte), 84
Wind's Bakery and Pasty Shop (Anaconda), 84

Cascade Meat Processors (Cascade), 34

Chalet Market (Belgrade), 18

Chaon's Game Processing (Great Falls), 34

Craig's Meat Processing Plant (Savage), 35.

5-D Processing (Choteau), 34

Forcella Meats (Whitehall), 33

Frey's Meat & Custom Cutting (Columbia Falls), 32

Gallatin Meat Processing (Bozeman), 33

Hamilton Packing Inc. (Hamilton), 33

Happel's Clean Cut Meat Service (Bozeman), 33

Heeb's East Main Grocery (Bozeman), 23

H&H Meats (Missoula), 33

Hi Country Beef Jerky (Lincoln), 33

Hi Line Meats (Glasgow), 35

Hoch Meat Processing (Wolf Point), 35

House of Meats Game Processing (Great Falls), 34

Lolo Locker (Lolo), 33

Lower Valley Processing Co. (Kalispell), 32

Matt's Old Fashioned Butcher Shop & Deli (Livingston), 30–31

The Meat Shoppe (Bozeman), 31

Montana Buffalo Gals (Dixon), 132

M & S Meats (Rollins), 130

North American Foods of Montana (Hamilton), 33

North Country Meats (Havre), 35

Pierce Meat Cutting (Sulphur Springs), 34

Roberts Packing Company (Dillon), 33

Rocky Mountain Packing (Havre), 35

Sage Brush Meats (Billings), 34

Sheep Mountain Meat Processing (Livingston), 33

Skip's Critter Cutting (Huntley), 35

Sportsman's Wild Game Processing (Great Falls), 34

Tizer Meats (Helena), 34

Tobacco Valley Meats (Eureka), 32

Top of the Hill Wild Game Processing (Polaris), 34

Trails End Meat Processing
(Billings), 35
Treasure Trail Processing
(Glasgow), 35
Tri-City Taxidermy & Wild Game
(Great Falls), 34
Valley Processing (Stevensville), 33
Vandevanter Meats, Inc. (Columbia
Falls), 32
Western Meats Wild Game
(Butte), 33
Yellowstone Processing
(Bozeman), 34

Natural Food Stores
Big Spring Market (Lewistown), 188
Community Food Co-Op
(Bozeman), 19
Foodworks (Livingston), 22
Good Earth Market (Billings), 235
Good Food Store (Missoula), 129
Missoula Community Food Co-op
(Missoula), 130–32
Oak Street Natural Market
(Bozeman), 27
Real Food Market & Deli
(Helena), 89

Sauces and Salsas
Babcock & Miles, Ltd. (Red
Lodge), 17
Sod House Sundries (Glendive),
239–40

Wines and Beer
Babcock & Miles, Ltd. (Red
Lodge), 17
Booze & Buns (Sheridan), 85
City Vineyard (Billings), 234
Front Street Market (Butte),
86–87
The Gourmet Cellar (Livingston),
22–23
Joe's Parkway Market
(Bozeman), 24
Plonk (Bozeman), 28
Simply Wine (Billings), 239
Toppers Cellar and Spirits
(Helena), 90–91
Uncorked Wines (Kalispell),
132–33
Vino per Tutti (Bozeman),
31–32, 36
The Wine Gallery (Bozeman),
29–30

Montana Eateries

Recipes Index

General Index

butcher shops, 30–31. *See also* meat processing plants

Butte, 75–76

railway, 81

Butte Farmers' Market, 92

C

Café Italia, 245

Café Regis, 48–49

Campfire Lodge Resort Café, 49

Candy Masterpiece, 189

Candy Town USA, Inc., 233–34

Canyon Lodge Dining Room, 70–71

Carter's Brewing, 254–55

Cascade Meat Processors, 34

Cattle-ac, 245

Chalet Market, 18

Chaon's Game Processing, 34

Charbonneau's Chocolate Shop, 128

cherries. *See* Flathead Lake Cherry Growers

Chico Hot Springs, 49, 52

recipe, 50–51

Chili Cook-off, 40–41

Chocolate Moose Candy Store and Soda Fountain, 18–19

Ciao Mambo, 150

Circle Farmers' Market, 212

City Vineyard, 234

Clark Fork Organics, 112–13

Clark Fork River Market, 133

The Coffee Cup, 189

The Coffee Den, 234

Coffee Factory Roasters, 19

Colter Coffee House and Roasting, 128

Columbus Farmers' Market, 240

Community Food Co-Op, 19

Continental Divide, 98

The Copper Colander, 234–35

The Copper Kettle Chocolates and Gem Gallery, 85

Copper King Express, 81

Country Classic Dairies, 4–5

Country Pasta, Inc., 113

recipe, 114

Cowboy Cuisine, Lake Hotel, 71

Craig's Meat Processing Plant, 35

D

Damascos Pizzeria and Spaghetteria, 52–53

Danly Farms, 224

About the Author

Seabring Davis is the editor in chief of *Big Sky Journal* magazine and editor in chief of *Western Art & Architecture* magazine. She is an award-winning journalist who writes about food, travel, western lifestyle, and art. The author of three books, including *A Montana Table: Recipes from Chico Hot Springs Resort* (Globe Pequot Press) and *Big Sky Journal's The New Montana Cabin* (Globe Pequot Press), she has lived in Montana for two decades and loves to cook with her family at their home in Livingston.